The Mental Health Capsule

Joshua Bess, Jane Anderson, Joelle Rabow Maletis, Nina Batista, Dr. Randi Reichel Fournier, Carley Symes

Talk+Tell

Distribution by KDP Amazon and Ingram Spark (P.O.D.)

Printed in the United States of America and Canada

Title: The Mental Health Capsule

Names: Joshua Bess, Jane Anderson, Joelle Rabow Maletis, Nina Batista, Randi Reichel Fournier, Carley Symes

Paperback ISBN: 9798272008596

Hardcover ISBN: 979-8-3482-9755-8

To you, the reader
for your courage to turn toward your own heart,
for every chapter you've survived,
and every step you've taken toward healing,
even on the days it felt impossible.
May these pages be a companion on your journey,
a light in the quiet places,
and a reminder that you are never beyond hope,
never beyond growth,
never beyond the possibility of beginning again.
This book is dedicated to your strength,
your softness,
your becoming,
and to the story you are still writing.

About the Authors

Chapter 2: Mapping Mental Health: A Journey with a Guide

By Joshua Bess, MD, Medical Director
Explores the mental health journey as a collaborative process, demystifying psychiatry's evolving role in balancing psychopharmacology, psychotherapy, and individualized care.

Chapter 3: Helping Others Heal from Loss: Navigating Grief and Rebuilding Hope

By Jane Anderson, MFS, CFLE
Shares personal and professional insights into understanding and supporting grief, offering tools for resilience and renewal.

Chapter 4: The Journey to Self-Love: Becoming Your Own Best Friend

By Joelle Rabow Maletis, MAEd, MA, LMFT
Celebrates the transformative power of self-love, offering strategies for embracing imperfections and fostering authenticity.

Chapter 5: The Labyrinth of Toxic Love: Recognizing and Reclaiming Yourself

By Nina Batista, MSW
Guides readers through recognizing toxic relationship patterns, breaking free, and reclaiming identity with self-compassion.

Chapter 6: A Recipe for a Fulfilling Intimate Life: Getting Comfortable with Uncomfortable Intimacy

By Dr. Randi Reichel Fournier, DMFT, LMFT, M.Ed.
Explores the complexities of sexual communication, intimacy, and growth through vulnerability and open conversation.

Chapter 7: Becoming Me: Letting Go of Perfection to Embrace Growth and Authenticity

By Carley Symes, BSc (Hons), MBACP

Explores the journey of self-discovery, emphasizing the importance of releasing societal expectations and embracing the evolving, imperfect versions of ourselves to foster genuine confidence and self-acceptance.

Introduction to The Mental Health Capsule

Mental health shapes every aspect of our lives. It influences how we wake in the morning, how we move through our days, how we relate to others, and how we understand ourselves. It dictates the quality of our relationships, the depth of our fulfillment, and the steadiness of our inner world. Even when we are not consciously thinking about it, mental health sits beneath every choice, every reaction, and every hope we hold for the future.

Yet for something so deeply woven into the human experience, mental health is often approached with hesitation. People worry that naming their struggles makes them weak. They fear that asking for help means something is fundamentally wrong with them. Many suffer quietly, believing their pain is too small to deserve attention or too large to be understood. Others have been taught to push forward at all costs, to perform strength rather than experience healing, to shrink their emotional needs so that they do not inconvenience anyone around them.

This anthology was created to offer a different way.

The Mental Health Capsule is a collection of voices committed to expanding what healing looks like, feels like, and requires. It brings together professionals from different disciplines who have devoted their lives to understanding the human mind, human emotion, and human resilience. Each contributor has sat with people during some of their darkest moments and has also witnessed the extraordinary strength that emerges when healing is met with compassion, knowledge, and the right support.

The purpose of this anthology is not to provide quick solutions or one size fits all answers. It is to illuminate the complexity of mental health with gentleness and clarity. It is to show how emotional wounds can shape a life and how healing can reshape it once more. It is to remind readers that they do not need to walk this journey alone. Understanding and support exist, and the insights shared in this book come from years of experience working with real people navigating real struggles.

This collection acknowledges something essential. Healing is not linear. Healing is not about perfection. Healing is not about eliminating every struggle. Healing is about learning who we are beneath fear, beneath grief, beneath shame, beneath the roles we were taught to play. It is about becoming more present in our own lives, more connected to our own needs, and more compassionate toward the parts of ourselves we once tried to ignore.

When people think about mental health, they often picture crisis points. Panic, depression, trauma, loss, burnout, heartbreak, or emotional numbing. But mental health also lives in quieter places. In the pressure to achieve. In the desire to be loved. In the belief that we must be everything for everyone. In the disappointment we carry from childhood into adulthood. In the expectations we place on ourselves to always be fine. Many people do not recognize they are struggling because they are so accustomed to functioning while hurting.

This anthology invites readers to slow down long enough to recognize what their minds and hearts have been whispering for years. It invites them to explore the roots of their emotional patterns and the stories they tell themselves about who they are allowed to be. It invites them to honor their pain without being swallowed by it. Most importantly, it invites them to imagine a healthier, fuller, more grounded version of themselves.

The contributors of *The Mental Health Capsule* have spent decades in the delicate space between evidence based practice and human experience. They understand that people do not heal from textbooks. They heal through connection. They heal through being seen and understood. They heal through knowledge delivered with compassion. They heal when they realize their story matters.

This anthology honors the full spectrum of what it means to be human. It acknowledges that the mind is complex and the heart is vulnerable. It recognizes that people often seek help when they feel they are falling apart, yet healing begins the moment someone says that their pain is valid. It also honors the courage of those who choose to heal before crisis forces them to. Healing is not only a response to suffering. It is an act of self respect.

Every person who contributed to this work believes deeply in the power of mental health education. They believe that people make better choices when they understand themselves. They believe that families grow stronger when emotional experiences are named rather than hidden. They believe that communities thrive when mental health is no longer stigmatized or misunderstood. They believe that access to knowledge is a form of empowerment that can change the trajectory of a life.

Their collective experiences reflect a simple, powerful truth. No matter how lost someone feels, healing is possible. Even when the path forward seems unclear. Even when the symptoms feel overwhelming. Even when shame convinces a person that they are too broken to be helped. Healing is always possible because the human spirit is profoundly resilient. People can learn. People can grow. People can change their relationships with themselves and the world around them.

Mental health is not a destination. It is an ongoing relationship with oneself. It requires honesty, curiosity, and patience. It requires learning how to listen to the body and the mind without judgment. It requires acknowledging the wounds we have carried, sometimes for decades, and giving ourselves permission to put them down. It requires setting boundaries that protect our emotional health rather than erode it. It requires self compassion, which for many is the hardest skill to develop.

This anthology honors the reality that healing looks different for everyone. For some, it begins with a diagnosis that finally explains what they have been feeling. For others, it begins with understanding grief in a new way. For others, it begins with conversations that deepen intimacy and trust. For others, it begins with letting go of perfectionism or rediscovering self love. Healing begins wherever a person finds the courage to look inward.

What makes *The Mental Health Capsule* unique is not only the expertise of its contributors, but the humanity behind their words. Their careers have placed them in the intimate space where people cry, break open, reveal the truth of their fears, and allow themselves to be vulnerable. They have witnessed the exact moment when someone realizes they are worthy of help. They have seen how emotional breakthroughs can transform families, relationships, careers, and futures.

They bring all of that lived wisdom into these pages. They write not only as professionals, but as people who understand how deeply mental health influences every corner of a life. Their perspectives come from sitting with the real world complexity of the human heart rather than speaking from theoretical distance. Their insight carries the weight of experience and the warmth of compassion.

The Mental Health Capsule is not meant to be read in one sitting. It is meant to be returned to. It is meant to be reflected on slowly. It is meant to stir questions inside the reader. It is meant to create space for new understanding. It is meant to open doors that may have remained closed for years.

Some readers will discover parts of themselves in these pages that they have not acknowledged before. Others will feel relief that their experiences finally have language. Others will gain tools that reshape how they communicate, how they love, and how they care for themselves. Others may find the courage to seek support for the first time. Still others may feel inspired not because they are struggling, but because they want to sustain a life that feels healthy and whole.

Mental health is not something we fix once and forget. It is something we tend to throughout our lives. It changes as we change. It evolves with new seasons, new relationships, new stressors, new environments, and new dreams. It requires a lifetime of gentle attention. This anthology supports that journey by offering perspectives that can meet readers at different stages of their lives.

The contributors of this anthology come from diverse training backgrounds and specialize in different parts of the mental health spectrum. Yet they share a belief that healing is possible, that vulnerability is powerful, and that informed support can change a person's life. Their work in this book stands as an offering to anyone searching for clarity, comfort, or a doorway to personal transformation.

The Mental Health Capsule is an invitation to slow down and listen. It is an invitation to honor the inner voice that has been quiet for too long. It is an invitation to ask important questions about identity, resilience, love, boundaries, grief, growth, and authenticity. It is an invitation to step toward a healthier future with greater understanding and compassion for yourself.

May these pages help you recognize the strength you already possess. May they provide comfort when you feel lost and guidance when you feel uncertain. May they encourage you to approach your own mind with kindness. And may they remind you that your story matters, your healing matters, and your well being deserves attention and care.

Welcome to *The Mental Health Capsule*. A space to learn. A space to heal. A space to become more fully yourself.

Contents

Chapter One

Mental Health Is Not One Size Fits All

Understanding the Many Ways We Heal and the Many Journeys We Walk

Mental health often gets spoken about as if it is a single experience with a single solution. People say things like "You should try this" or "This worked for my friend" or "Everyone feels that way sometimes" as if there is one correct way to struggle and one correct way to heal. This belief is something most of us absorb without ever questioning it. It lives quietly in the background of many conversations, shaping the way we judge our progress and the way we compare ourselves to others.

But the reality is far more intricate, far more layered, and far more compassionate.

Mental health is not one size fits all. It never has been. It never could be. Human beings are far too diverse in experience, temperament, culture, biology, identity, memory, and meaning for our emotional worlds to follow the same script. The inner life of a person is shaped by thousands of unseen influences. Each one of us carries a story that no one else has lived. Each one of us has an emotional language that no one else has spoken. Each one of us has a nervous system that reacts in its own unique pattern. Every mind forms its own architecture.

When you look closely at people, you begin to see that there is no single way to break and no single way to mend. Some people fall apart quietly. Some erupt loudly. Some hide their struggles behind a practiced smile. Some cannot speak without crying. Some seek closeness. Some withdraw. Some feel anxious. Some feel numb. Some feel everything at once. Some feel nothing at all. And all of these responses are valid. All of them are human. All of them make sense when understood through the lens of that person's life.

What heals one person may feel ineffective to another. What feels grounding to one person may feel suffocating to someone else. What brings insight to one may bring confusion to another. There is no single key that unlocks every door. Healing takes different forms, just as suffering takes different forms.

The Myth of the Standard Journey

There is a common fantasy that if we follow the right steps, we will arrive at the right destination. The steps change depending on whom we listen to, but the fantasy remains the same. Do this and you will feel better. Think this way and your anxiety will vanish. Heal this wound and your relationships will flow. Name this pattern and it will dissolve. Talk about your pain and it will evaporate. Rest and you will rise. Move forward and the past will release its grip.

Sometimes this is true. Often it is not. Healing is not an instruction manual. It is a relationship with oneself that grows and shifts as life grows and shifts. There are seasons when clarity comes easily and seasons when every answer feels out of reach. There are moments when a single insight transforms everything and moments when a hundred conversations change nothing. There are days when the soul opens and days when it closes. There are phases of progress and phases of returning to older patterns. The journey does not move in one direction. It expands and contracts. It circles. It pauses. It breaks open. It integrates.

The greatest misunderstanding people have about mental health is the belief that progress is supposed to look like a straight line. But healing rarely moves forward in neat increments. Instead, it moves like weather. It shifts. It repeats. It surprises. It cycles back through old terrain, not because you have failed, but because you are revisiting what could not be fully understood before. Returning is part of moving forward.

A Landscape Shaped by Many Forces

To understand your mental health is to understand the many forces that shape your inner life. No single event explains everything about you. No single feeling defines you. You are the accumulation of every experience, every memory, every environment, every relationship, every moment of safety, every moment of fear, every expectation placed on you, every identity you have tried on, and every belief you have inherited or rejected.

You are shaped by culture, family, gender roles, trauma, biology, opportunity, injustice, desire, loneliness, love, and every place where your heart has been touched or wounded. Some people grow up with encouragement. Some grow up with survival. Some grow up with affection. Some grow up with silence. These early patterns create the emotional templates that influence adulthood.

Your mind responds to the world through the shape of your history.

This is why two people can walk through the same door and emerge with entirely different experiences. One person may remember feeling supported. Another may remember feeling unsafe. One may feel hopeful in a crisis. Another may feel frozen. One may trust easily. Another may trust no one. These responses do not reflect character or strength. They reflect wiring that was shaped long before conscious choice existed.

Why Healing Looks Different for Everyone

Because mental health is shaped by so many factors, the way we heal must honor these differences. Some people find healing through reflection and insight. They grow through understanding the origins of their patterns. Others heal through action, movement, and sensation. Their bodies hold stories their minds cannot yet speak. Some learn through connection. Some learn through solitude. Some need structure. Some need freedom. Some need time. Some need intensity. Some need gentleness. Some need to revisit the past. Some need to reimagine the future.

No one way is superior. No one way is universal.

Growth looks different depending on your nervous system, personality, history, and the resources you have available. Someone with a lifetime of safety may find vulnerability refreshing. Someone with a lifetime of fear may find vulnerability threatening. Someone who has always been believed may speak openly. Someone who has been dismissed may speak cautiously. Someone who is used to emotional closeness may find separation frightening. Someone who is used to emotional distance may find closeness overwhelming.

Healing must be tailored to the person, not the other way around.

The Field of Mental Health Reflects This Diversity

Although we are not listing professions here, it is important to acknowledge something essential. The mental health field itself is full of diverse practitioners who specialize in different areas for a reason. No single perspective can meet every need. No single approach captures the entire human experience. Practitioners choose different methods because they recognize that people require different forms of support.

This diversity is not a flaw. It is a gift. It means you will always be able to find someone whose way of understanding aligns with your way of being. It means there is room for every story.

It means your lived experience matters. It means there is a place for the specific kind of care you require.

Building Your Own Map

If mental health is not one size fits all, then you are invited to build your own map. Not a map drawn from comparison or expectation or cultural rules. Not a map made from someone else's life. A map that emerges from your own landscape. A map that honors who you are, what you carry, and what you need.

This map may include reflection. It may include rest. It may include movement, community, boundaries, medication, nature, conversation, ritual, creative expression, stillness, or finding meaning in places others overlook. The map may change as you change. The map may expand as you expand. It may require you to release old beliefs about what it means to be strong, good, successful, or worthy.

Healing is not about becoming someone else. It is about returning to yourself. It is about recognizing the parts of you that were silenced, dismissed, or ignored. It is about learning to listen to the wisdom that lives inside your body. It is about trusting your instincts, even when they lead you into unfamiliar territory. It is about nurturing the parts of you that never received care. It is about understanding that you do not need to earn rest, tenderness, or ease.

Most importantly, healing is about reconnecting with your own humanity.

Your Journey Is Yours Alone

There will be people who try to tell you what your healing should look like. They may judge your pace. They may misunderstand your needs. They may pressure you to heal quickly or quietly. But your journey does not owe anyone clarity or speed. You are not a project. You are not a checklist of symptoms. You are not a schedule that someone else can design.

Your healing is not meant to be understood by everyone. Your healing is meant to be lived by you.

The Truth at the Center of It All

If there is one idea I want you to carry from this chapter, it is this:

There is nothing wrong with you for needing something different.

There is nothing wrong with you for not responding to what worked for others. There is nothing wrong with you for taking longer. There is nothing wrong with you for needing gentleness when others need structure. There is nothing wrong with you for finding your path through intuition rather than logic. There is nothing wrong with you for struggling in ways that others do not understand.

Your mental health journey is not meant to match anyone else's experience. It is meant to match your life, your history, your body, your mind, and your heart.

And that is not a limitation. It is a profound truth about what it means to be human.

You are allowed to heal in the way that makes sense for you. You are allowed to seek support that fits your story. You are allowed to create a new identity after loss or trauma. You are allowed to grow in directions no one expected. You are allowed to take all the time you need. You are allowed to choose yourself again and again.

You are not too much. You are not too complicated. You are not too slow. You are not too sensitive. You are not behind. You are becoming.

And becoming looks different for everyone.

Chapter Two

Mapping Mental Health: A Journey with a Guide

By Joshua Bess MD, Medical Director

A highly respected psychiatrist and the Medical Director at the Seattle Neuropsychiatric Treatment Center (NTC), specializing in brain stimulation therapies like ECT and TMS for treatment-resistant mood disorders, depression, OCD, and catatonia.

People seeking mental health* find themselves on quite the journey. For many, the mental health journey is lifelong. And no one starts with the whole map; it's more like the "mini map" in the corner of a video game screen... you must move toward a blurred/dark edge to reveal more of the path ahead.

Embarking on the Mental Health Journey

Every mental health journey has parts which must be completed alone. Most have sections which are discovered with the help of one or a few companions. And some parts of some mental health journeys involve a whole team of people on the journey with you, or even a whole community traveling together.

Mental health *treatment** is also a trek - it's called a "course" of treatment after all. It is *within* the overall mental health journey. Treatment is only *part* of the larger map to mental health. How much of the path to mental health involves treatment depends on the person. For some, treatment might be the only bridge across a raging river, with some sort of horrible beasts giving chase. For others it could be one of several paths from which to choose, any of which can illuminate the next part of the map. In the best circumstances, treatment helps a person reach their destination safely, and perhaps more quickly than without it. Even then, it is a challenge all on its own and, while important and necessary, can consume a lot of time and energy. On the other hand, in some cases, treatment can be a side-quest that accomplishes nothing toward the bigger mission, veers far from the main road, and wastes time and resources.

The sheer number of treatment options is intimidating, like in a video game, e.g. *The Legend of Zelda: Tears of the Kingdom*. It can feel overwhelming. An open world adventure like that technically has infinite choices, right? [Breznitz, 1984] Perhaps it is more helpful to compare the treatment journey to something less complex – say, the original *Legend of Zelda* from the 1980s. Or even better, a *Choose Your Own Adventure* book from that same era. There are many choices, but the number of paths is finite and some of them overlap. There are also clues along the way about what treasure or danger lurks ahead.

A guide can be helpful! This is where I come in.

I am a psychiatrist. In the US, becoming a psychiatrist usually involves graduating from college with a bachelor's degree then attending 4 years of medical school. During the final year of medical school, students choose a specialty then apply for residency spots in that specialty. (That *also* sounds a lot like some sort of video game... maybe more like *The Sims*!)

My medical school classmates dispersed into dozens of residency programs across many specialties, for example general surgery, internal medicine, obstetrics and gynecology, or radiology. Eight of us, out of 250, chose to do residency in psychiatry. A standard psychiatry residency is 4 years *after* medical school, after which a person is qualified as a general psychiatrist (a.k.a.

adult psychiatrist). There is also the option for *additional* training after residency, called fellowship, if someone wants to have an even more specific focus. Examples here include child/adolescent psychiatry or forensic psychiatry. Fellowship adds on an extra year or more.

So, a guide like me, a psychiatrist, is a medical doctor, a.k.a. a physician, with a college degree, a medical degree, then 4 (or more) additional years of specialty training in the field of psychiatry. And I am setting aside all the people who have other training besides that, like my friends who graduated from an MD/PhD program, or those who pursue a master's in public health (MPH).

Discovering My Why

Now you know *how* I got this gig, but you might be wondering "why?" My choice to specialize in psychiatry has a lot to do with why I continue to work in the field today. The short answer: 1) I liked the psychiatrists I worked with in medical school and residency; and 2) I found out I was good at it. I entered medical school planning to be a pediatrician or family doctor. Those were the only types of physicians I had encountered to that point in my life, the only examples I had. The University of Michigan Medical School in the early 2000s had a traditional curriculum structure in that the first two "pre-clinical" years were mostly lectures and small groups, then the 3rd and 4th years were "clinical" – on hospital wards and in medical offices.

My first inkling that I might want to be a psychiatrist came when I worked at a community mental health clinic with Timothy Florence MD. He had a mastery of the complexities of people's psychiatric medications, awareness of the psychosocial contributors to their difficult situations, and unrelenting, but realistic, optimism that people's situations could improve. But most influential to me was his style of engaging with clients – very unassuming, non-judgmental, and warm. I discovered that I had a similar style. And, as I emulated some of the finer points of my mentor's interview skills, people started to trust me and tell me what was bothering them.

By early adulthood I had never met a psychiatrist. Many of you probably haven't either! For many people, especially those who have never met a *real* psychiatrist, the term recalls media portrayals. Some of these, like Dr. Jennifer Melfi on *The Sopranos* or Dr. Frasier Crane on *Cheers* and *Frasier* (and the new *Frasier* reboot), have become cultural touchstones. Many of the more well-known psychiatrists in the media act primarily as psychotherapists, which perhaps contributes to an overall misconception that we all have that same job description. We do not.

The Evolution of Psychiatry

Psychiatry as a separate specialty started with the custodial care of individuals in mental asylums in the 1800s and the first part of the 1900s. [Shorter, 1997] But, by World War II, psychiatry evolved in response to the huge influence of psychoanalysis, a.k.a. "the talking cure." Enter the classic *New Yorker* cartoon with someone (or maybe a dog) lying on the couch in a psychiatrist's office. The first question I am asked when someone learns I am a psychiatrist is "Do you have a couch in your office?" (I do not.) As mentioned, this is *historically* accurate. But, while there are still psychiatrists who practice primarily psychotherapy, most of them do not even have a therapy couch in their office either, opting instead for comfortable armchairs or a sofa (on which people sit).

This skewing of media depictions makes sense, since the discussion of difficult topics in therapy, the chance to see the psychiatrist as an engaged human, and the growth and healing that can happen in psychotherapy makes for good TV (or New Yorker cartoons)! Moreover, the ethically questionable and/or unprofessional relationships sometimes depicted between these fictional psychiatrists and their clients/clients' associates – as might happen when you are working with a mob boss – also can be exciting entertainment.

The further evolution of psychiatry *since* the middle of the 20th century has been exciting in different ways, perhaps not as "ready for prime time." There were ground-breaking advances in psychopharmacology in the 1950s and 1960s. Before that the medication armamentarium mostly consisted of opium, barbiturates (strong sedatives) and amphetamines. In fact, the latter 2 were available in combination pills – yes, an upper and a downer – for example Dexamyl. *[Healy, 1997]*. The 1950s saw development of the first antipsychotic medication, chlorpromazine (Thorazine) and the first antidepressant medication, isoniazid. (The *psychiatric* effects of both were discovered somewhat by accident.)

Early psychiatric medications had significant side effects and were often very dangerous or lethal if taken in large quantities, so they were reserved for those with severe illness and very carefully monitored, often by a psychiatrist who was also providing intensive psychotherapy. The medication was considered a tool to help the person do the therapy work. Even though the pharmaceutical was not the "main treatment," the groundwork was being laid for more liberal prescribing of medications for depression, anxiety, and psychosis – among other mental health troubles.

Through the 1970s and into the 1980s, somewhat safer medications were developed, and the emphasis started to lean toward a "chemical cure" for some people. With the explosion of SSRI medications onto the scene, starting with fluoxetine (Prozac) in 1987, antidepressants were very safe, even in overdose. Along with another game-changer – HMO insurance – the SSRIs and other medications started to be seen as the primary treatment, even the "cure," themselves instead of only as an adjunct to the "real work" of psychotherapy. Seeing a psychiatrist and walking out with a prescription

became an expectation on both sides of the treatment relationship. Throw in the increased influence of biological approaches and research methods in the 1980s and 1990s (the

1990s were the "Decade of the Brain" after all) *[American Psychiatric Association, 1994]*, and the takeover of academic psychiatry departments by biologically oriented faculty (who were training the next generation of psychiatrists), and the evolution took on some characteristics of a revolution... or at least some moderate upheaval of the status quo!

The politics and financial incentives involved in this transformation are interesting, and parts feel downright smarmy, but a full exploration of that is outside of the scope of this chapter. *[Whitaker, 2002]*

Suffice it to say, medications are cheaper than psychotherapy (especially psychotherapy delivered by a psychiatrist), brain scans are sexier than obtuse-seeming psychodynamic theories, and psychiatrists, for the most part, enjoy being treated as "real physicians" delivering "medical treatment." To put it more simply, over the last half of the 20th century there was a transformation in how typical psychiatrists spend their time.

The current day reality has outpaced the most media portrayals as described above. Fictional psychiatrists rarely talk about medication, at least not in the detailed way we real ones must explain them to make sure the person taking them is giving informed consent. Even outpatient psychiatrists who offer a balanced approach of talk therapy *and* medications are also going to spend significant time discussing side effects, possible interactions with other medications (psychiatric or otherwise), a person's other "physical" medical problems, and the blood tests and EKGs necessary to maintain safety parameters or monitor medication side effects. And this does *not* make for good TV! It sounds more like the legalese at the end of a pharmaceutical commercial.

The Art and Science of Psychiatric Decision-Making

On the other hand, practicing psychiatry is not just advanced chemistry, no matter what those pharmaceutical commercials might have you believe. There is a lot of focus in advertisements on which medication(s) might fix one's anxiety or depression, but something else that gets glossed over is the complex decisions about whether medication is appropriate in the first place. This is one very important way in which we psychiatrists act as a guide on the treatment journey. There are a lot of nuances involved, especially when considering the risks of a particular medication path.

Often the right decision is to avoid the medication path altogether. But when it comes to prescribing medication, particularly ones that are heavily advertised or helped someone our client is close to, we often find it challenging to say "no" and explain why a certain course of treatment is not warranted. A mentor of mine once told me, "It takes 30 seconds to say 'yes' and 30 minutes to say 'no.'" The difficulty arises from various factors, including the complex dynamics of medical care, the desire to alleviate suffering, and the potential for conflict or dissatisfaction from clients. We are trained to treat and alleviate symptoms, and when someone presents with anxiety, which is something that a controlled substance like a benzodiazepine can often quickly and effectively address, we are inclined to provide relief. It feels very strange not to! But we must balance the desire to help with the responsibility to consider the overall health and well-being of the people we treat. Sometimes *that* means *not* prescribing certain medications. It means leading someone away from what looks (deceivingly) like the "easy" path.

Saying "no" and the related complexities are part of many interactions, not only around certain medications. Informed consumers who have seen repeated commercials where the clouds turn to sunshine, with the voiceover explaining the high percentage of people who were helped by the medication, are going to have an idea about what they need before the appointment with their psychiatrist is even made. But a major part of our job is to help people sort through the information that is presented in advertisements and other media, to explain why something might be helpful or might not. Especially challenging are cases where the diagnosis includes subjective criteria, like much of psychiatry. Saying "no" not only requires careful clinical judgment but also the ability to effectively communicate and manage expectations.

Where might you find one of these psychiatrist-guides to help you uncover more of the map? I have discussed how many fictional psychiatrists primarily as psychotherapists, which in fact only represents a minority of real-world colleagues of mine. [Shorter, 1997] Many psychiatrists, especially in outpatient private practice, spend 45-50 minutes with each client and provide a combination of "medication management" and psychotherapy. For those who participate in insurance, these are coded separately, with the "medical" part as the primary code and the psychotherapy as an "add-on." Finally, there are some practicing psychiatrists who, like me, focus *primarily* on the medication or other "biological" treatments and do little or no formal psychotherapy with the people we see.

In the 2020s there are numerous places and ways that a psychiatrist can practice. It is a matter of

who you work for,
who your co-workers are,
who your clients are,
where your work is done, and
what you do during those visits.

who we work for
who our co-workers are
who our clients are
where our work is done
what we do during those visits

self
no one
certain problems or diagnoses
single office/virtual
ongoing psychotherapy + some medications
small clinic/org
share space with a few people

level of acuity or severity

private office with other private offices in the same building

ongoing medications + brief/infrequent psychotherapy

large clinic/org

larger care team w/ other providers

needing specific interventions

private office or shared office in a multi-provider single-specialty practice

ongoing combination of meds and regular psychotherapy

hospital/health system

+/- office staff, nurses, attendants, technicians, etc

by virtue of where they work, live, study, get other care

primary care clinic or other specialty clinic (eg oncology, infectious disease)

other interventions (TMS, ECT)

government institution

by virtue of being treated in the hospital for something else

general medical or surgical floor of a regular hospital

single/few visit(s) evaluation/diagnosis

psychiatric unit in a regular (general) hospital

co-management with another provider

free-standing psychiatric hospital

administration

government facility like a jail/prison, school system

Where Psychiatrists Practice: A Spectrum of Roles

Psychiatrists are some of the last physician holdouts in the world of "private practice," where one has an office (virtual and/or real) and makes all the decisions about how to run the practice. This can mean either working alone or with other psychiatrists, psychologists, therapists, nurse practitioners, physician assistants, etc – more on that below. On the other hand, an increasing number of psychiatrists are employed by larger organizations, either hospitals/healthcare systems or multi-site group practices. The private-practice or employed-by-a-clinic psychiatrist would be a guide you likely need to seek out, maybe based on reputation or seeing an advertisement, or maybe one who was recommended by a friend or another doctor.

There has always been a cadre working in government institutions as well, like prisons, jails (some of which are the largest mental health providers in their geographic area), state hospitals (they do still exist!), or community mental health centers. Some of these psychiatrists are asked to help someone who has not requested the help. That can be a very tricky situation indeed.

Some psychiatrists still provide primarily psychotherapy, as discussed above, maybe with some "medication management" as *part* of the treatment plan. This is especially common in private practice. Most of these do not participate, or participate very minimally, in insurance plans since insurance companies [Whitaker, 2002] do not reimburse psychotherapy as well as more "medical" interventions (also discussed above). Some of my colleagues see many clients each day for 10-, 15- or 20-minute "medication checks." This model is increasingly common in larger practices, community mental health centers, and other settings which operate on insurance reimbursement or public funding. Medications *can* be very helpful, and, with the increased use of symptom rating scales and evidence-based algorithms, meaningful care can be provided in this model.

Some psychiatrists work in free-standing psychiatric hospitals or the psychiatric unit (a.k.a. "psych ward") at a general hospital. They work with people whose psychiatric illness is so severe that they are not safe at home or able to care for themselves. Some work on a "consultation-liaison" service, seeing those who have a psychiatric component or side-effect to the medical or surgical problem for which they are admitted to the general hospital. Some psychiatrists work in emergency departments or specialized psychiatric emergency services. We are frequently tapped for medical administration roles, perhaps because we are used to talking to people in depth. Many psychiatrists practice in more than one setting; one of the wonderful things about the field is the variety of roles one can assume.

Some of us are generalists, some are sub-sub-specialists, with the rest in between. Some concentrate on populations, e.g., children, women, peripartum women, people with cancer, people who have had organ transplants, people who are unhoused, etc. Some focus on certain diagnoses, e.g., psychosis/schizophrenia, OCD, treatment-resistant mood disorders, autism spectrum disorder, etc. Some psychiatrists see "all comers," for example the psychiatrist in the emergency department of a busy urban hospital. Others carefully screen requests to make sure they have the time and expertise to help the people accepted into their care. Many of us teach, maybe as "core" (employed) faculty at a medical school or academic medical center or as "adjunct" faculty (where students or residents come to our practice to work with us, but we are not employed by the medical school or academic medical center). Others teach more informally, offering advice to colleagues in different fields, working on multi-disciplinary teams, writing blogs or posting on social media, or supervising non-physician advanced practice providers (APPs, eg nurse practitioners or physician assistants, for whom level of independence in practice varies by state).

Part of what makes psychiatrists such useful guides on the journey toward mental health is that we are adaptable and flexible. You come to us or we meet you where you are. If you need a guide with a different set of skills than me, I can help you find that person. The extensive training we receive helps with this process as well. "Maybe I do not work with people on your specific type of journey right now, but I used to and I know how to get you started and who can help you further."

It is relatively rare to find two psychiatrists with the same job description! My fellow guides are equipped to help people with different parts of their treatment journey. It is a very nice feature for people who work in this field, since we can settle into a comfortable niche and/or change things up as often as we like to keep it interesting. But we also understand that it can be very confusing and disappointing for the people we are trying to help.

-"Dr. Bess, I really like working with you. Can you be my psychotherapist?"

-"No, sorry. I don't have that kind of expertise."

-"Can you work with my son? He is having trouble adjusting to 6th grade."

-"No, sorry, but I have some colleagues who might be helpful."

-"If I run into another adult who needs this intensity of intervention for their medication-resistant depression can I tell them you might be able to help?"

-Definitely!"

For 5 years after psychiatry training, I worked in a large academic hospital - on the inpatient psychiatry unit, on the consultation-liaison service, on the electroconvulsive therapy (ECT) team, and in Psychiatric Emergency Services (PES). I was a core faculty member, teaching pre-clinical medical students, medical students on clinical rotations, and residents who were training in psychiatry.

For the last 10 years I have been a sub-specialist outpatient psychiatrist in a multi-clinic single-specialty group practice (which I partly own) in an urban area and its surrounds. Our sub-specialty is treatment-resistant depression and other treatment-resistant mental illnesses, specifically involving interventional psychiatry treatments like electroconvulsive therapy (ECT), transcranial magnetic stimulation (TMS), intranasal esketamine (Spravato®), intravenous ketamine, vagus nerve stimulation (VNS), and others. I also prescribe medications for mood disorders, psychosis, anxiety, OCD, and ADHD. I still teach psychiatry residents, now as an *adjunct* faculty member. My colleagues and I do didactic sessions for 2nd-year residents, while 3rd- and 4th-year residents work in our clinic 1 day per week.

Do we still want what a typical day looks like?

While I do not advertise myself as a psychotherapist, I do believe that every interaction between a healer and a person seeking to be healed can be therapeutic. Furthermore, I know that even when we feel like we are "out of ideas" or "don't have an answer" for someone, we can be present and bear witness to their distress or suffering as we work together to figure out what the next step might be. Sometimes that next step is *reducing* medication or *stopping* an interventional treatment or taking a break from treatment altogether to regroup. I often remind people that this treatment journey can be like a full-time job, and sometimes you need a vacation! There are times when the next step is referring someone to a practitioner who heals in ways I do not claim to understand, encouraging a person to seek out spiritual guidance, or convincing them to try a new therapist or counselor even though "therapy doesn't work" for them.

I readily admit when I don't know the answer, and either I recommend someone who does or offer to help the person in their search. I do not dismiss peoples' experiences – positive or negative – with medications, treatments, or life as "just coincidence." I can advise when "as far as we know" something is not "a thing" but that new "things" happen all the time.

It is important to specifically discuss all of the different kinds of guides one may run into on a mental health treatment journey. Psychiatrists are just one category of people who work in "mental health" or "behavioral health" treatment. Navigating the system, you may also encounter other professionals, such as psychologists, psychotherapists, nurse practitioners, physician assistants, pharmacists, nurses, medical assistants, technicians, speech therapists, occupational therapists, and other kinds of therapists. There are other physicians who, though not trained in psychiatry, prescribe psychiatric medications for depression or anxiety or other things. There are practitioners of "traditional" or "non-Western," or "complimentary/alternative" healing arts who are very important members of some people's treatment teams.

You might encounter these mental health professionals in a mental health clinic, in a hospital, on Zoom, in your home, at a health fair, in a homeless encampment, in your primary care physician's office, in jail or prison, at your workplace, or at your church. And there are even mental health professionals trying to help you who you might never meet, working at your insurance company, behind the scenes in your primary care providers office, or in a large health system or government agency, tracking behavioral health "data" and "outcomes."

Illustrating the Mental Health Journey Through Examples

I think some specific examples could also help illustrate the ideas I am trying to convey. There are many problems with the diagnostic approach in psychiatry and medicine in general, but for now it is the language most people speak. When seeking help, starting a mental health/treatment journey, some people have a problem (or one or more "symptoms") and they want clarification, maybe a diagnosis, to be able to explain why. Others have received a diagnosis already and are looking for a guide to get them to/through the next steps, hopefully finding relief, comfort, and return to their "normal" life along the way.

Depression:

Starting Point: Perhaps surprising to those who have seen it, I think *Ted Lasso* has a very helpful portrayal of depression. Star player Danny is introduced as almost absurdly upbeat and optimistic. A tragedy for which he feels responsible immediately flips the script. What is illustrative here is that the feelings of guilt, sadness, and pessimism completely swamp Danny and severely impair his ability to function as a person and an athlete. Yes, there was a distinct "trigger" for this depression, which is not always the case (but can be... it took me a long time to learn that depression triggered by an event sometimes is "real" depression, not necessarily just sadness or grief).

Journey Toward Help: Danny was offered support from teammates and, of course, Coach Lasso. The team hired a psychologist who met with Danny individually and was very helpful. While the show did not portray Danny taking antidepressant medication, that could have been considered as an option as well. Other important aspects to Danny's recovery, facilitated by his occupation, were establishing a routine, exercise, and self-care practices.

Other comments: Since I discussed problematic portrayals of therapeutic relationships above, I should point out that there are some "boundary violations," nothing salacious, involving Coach Lasso and the psychologist later in the series.

Anxiety Disorders:

Starting Point: The short film *Anxiety's Wilma (2019)* vividly portrays the daily struggles of a character named Wilma, offering a glimpse into the overwhelming effects of anxiety on someone's daily life. Even the title suggests how the film shows how anxiety can "possess" someone, take control of them and their actions.

Journey Toward Help: Wilma sees a therapist. Though it is unclear in the film whether she is finding therapy helpful at the moment, we also see Wilma grounding herself in reality, then confronting the anxiety. These are helpful skills that can be learned and rehearsed in formal psychotherapy, but also from articles, books, or videos (such as *Anxiety's Wilma*)! Cognitive-behavioral therapy (CBT) is especially effective in treating anxiety. Medications, lifestyle changes, and mindfulness practices can be helpful. Developing coping strategies, such as deep breathing exercises, is also beneficial.

Other Comments: Particularly intriguing in this piece are the very negative, hurtful ways in which Anxiety speaks to Wilma. It is not just about being nervous or scared.

Bipolar Disorder:

Starting Point: The 2014 film *Infinitely Polar Bear* captures the complexities of bipolar disorder through the characters of Cam, a father navigating manic highs and depressive lows, and Maggie, a mother who is pursuing a master's degree to provide better opportunities for their daughters. As Maggie focuses on her studies, Cam takes on the responsibility of caring for the girls full-time. Despite his love for his daughters, Cam's unpredictable behavior and emotional volatility make it difficult for him to fulfill his role as a father.

Journey Toward Help: Cam's illness is severe at times, to the point where he needs inpatient hospitalization to assure his safety and get him intensive treatment. A mainstay of his recovery is a mood-stabilizer medication, lithium, which can be very effective but also cause significant side-effects. Cam spends a lot of time not taking his lithium, which is a very realistic portrayal of the struggles someone might have with this illness and its treatments. Other helpful interventions with bipolar disorder include therapy (including psychoeducation) and support groups. Regular monitoring and management of medications are crucial. Lifestyle adjustments, such as maintaining a consistent sleep schedule and daily routine, are also recommended.

Other Comments: Bipolar disorder can destroy families. This film highlights the strain on familial bonds, not only Cam, Maggie, and their daughters but also Cam and his family of origin. It also showcases the resilience that can be found within family relationships.

Eating Disorders:

Starting Point: A film which delves into the intricacies of eating disorders is *To the Bone* (2017). The story is told from the point of view of Ellen, whose journey with anorexia sheds light on the physical and emotional toll it can take, the challenges of recovery, and the importance of self-acceptance.

Journey Toward Help: Eating disorders, especially anorexia nervosa, often require intensive *medical* treatment as well as psychiatric/psychological interventions, including medical hospitalization in severe cases. The film shows Ellen "failing" at various programs. The treatment journey she takes with the guidance of Dr. Beckham is "non-traditional" in some ways, but this illustrates the creativity that is often required to be able to help people who have not found "traditional" methods useful. The involvement of peers is important, especially in this type of illness where people can be very isolated. Family therapy is often emphasized since they are needed for ongoing support and are often suffering along with the person with an eating disorder.

Other Comments: The very complex physiology and psychology of eating disorders makes it very tricky to portray them in film. Trigger warnings are appropriate in general, and especially with a film about a person with anorexia like *To the Bone*.

Schizophrenia:

Starting Point: The first movie to pop into most people's mind when you say "schizophrenia" is *A Beautiful Mind* (2001). In many ways it is an excellent depiction of the struggle someone has between the life they want and the illness they are fighting. However, I think a more realistic example is *Canvas* (2006). The main character, Mary, has schizophrenia. Her goals are to have meaningful relationships with her husband and her young son. The context laid out around her is believable because we all know people like Mary.

Journey Toward Help: Medications fail Mary, as they often do in situations like hers. It is a powerful reminder that, while very useful, medications do not cure anything. Like Cam in *Infinitely Polar Bear,* Mary must go to the hospital in order to have the extra help and support she needs to get back on the road to recovery. We also see the toll that an illness like this takes on the other members of the family.

Other Comments: It is impossible to find the "perfect" depiction of a set of problems in film or other media... not only because of the artistic license involved in making it an engaging piece of art, but also because each person's set of circumstances is unique, just like their journey to mental health treatment. But these examples can be helpful as part of the map; illustrations about what the journey might look like at various points.

As we wrap up this overview of psychiatrist-guides, I am reminded that, along with my professional colleagues, mental health "writ large" is portrayed in movies, TV shows, and books in problematic ways. It's often oversimplified or overdramatized, creating misunderstandings and stigma. But that is a chapter for another day... let's focus on the positive.

Thinking about seeking help for mental health, it's a bit like navigating through a video game or a "Choose Your Own Adventure" book. It's a diverse and challenging journey, full of unexpected twists and turns, with different paths and guides along the way. Just like characters in games, individuals navigating mental health challenges can encounter diverse experiences and unexpected victories. Every person's journey to mental well-being is unique.

My goal here was to show the diverse ways people can seek help for their mental health, and especially the guides who can assist them. By comparing this journey to a game or a story, I want to highlight the various paths available and the roles of different helpers in the process. Just like characters in a game or a book, individuals navigating mental health challenges can try out different approaches and resources. My focus on psychiatrists and psychiatric treatments serve as the primary example for three reasons: 1) it is what I know, 2) it is an important piece that many people do not have access to, and 3) it is misunderstood and stigmatized.

Despite the challenges, the key message here is one of hope and empowerment. By recognizing the diverse array of helpers and resources available in the realm of mental health, individuals can approach their journey with a sense of possibility and agency. Every step taken in the pursuit of mental well-being can offer opportunities for growth, healing, and resilience, much like the diverse adventures found in games and stories.

**Definitions of terms in this arena – e.g., "mental health," behavioral health," "brain health," "mental illness," "psychiatric illness," "mental health care," "treatment," "psychiatric care," "patient," "client," "sick," "well" – are debated, complex, context-dependent, loaded, full of assumptions, conflicting, and/or clichéd. This chapter is about my view of mental health, illness, and treatment, and the role of someone like me as a guide in this weird world. I have embraced the ambiguity and imperfection of the terms used to explain ideas here and ask readers to do the same.*

Chapter Three

Helping Others Heal from Loss: Navigating Grief and Rebuilding Hope

By Jane Anderson, MFS, CFLE

A seasoned educator and crisis expert, ignites change through impactful training on mental health and family life.

Throughout my childhood, my parents volunteered at the local mission. They often shared heartfelt stories of the loss they observed which led to feelings of desperation experienced by those residing in the shelter. It was not long before I accompanied them on distinct occasions and there were even instances when a mission resident would be invited to our home on a special holiday. Looking back, I did not fully comprehend what true homelessness and loss meant to the victim of such a circumstance, but I do remember wanting to help and feeling compelled to be involved. It was not until I became a teen that I found myself on one winter afternoon thrust into a new reality, one that shattered the walls of detachment I had built around the narratives of others.

Recognizing Loss:

I can vividly recall that day as my family and I were deep in preparations at home as we readied for the upcoming Christmas holiday. My siblings and I were fervently engaged in the joyous task of adorning our tree. The air was filled with the harmonious tunes of Christmas carols, and the scent of freshly cut wintergreen danced around us. The festive atmosphere, however, took a profound turn as we left our comfortable home and traveled to the local rescue mission to wrap gifts for the families staying in the shelter. Little did I comprehend the transformative journey that awaited me, a passage that would expose me to the raw and unfiltered truths of hardship and loss.

Stepping into the mission, we were greeted by a room filled with donated items, haphazardly organized by age and gender. These items, intended for those in residence or seeking Christmas assistance, were not mere tokens of generosity but rather practical necessities that adults needed. The donated toys lacked the personal touch that fulfills a child's Christmas dreams and most gifts were intended to meet a child's basic needs and left much to be desired.

As a curious teen, I ventured out to wander the adjoining rooms. I was drawn by the noise in the dining hall where mothers and their children were seated. The tables were trimmed with holiday colors, and soft Christmas music provided a backdrop as families formed lines at the buffet. While the portions were generous, the choices were starkly limited. Seated at a table, I overheard children eagerly discussing Santa's imminent visit, their eyes brimming with hope. However, the coveted toys they spoke of were noticeably absent from the pile of gifts being wrapped by volunteers. I remember that there were hundreds of toys, yet most were generic and certainly did not align with the list of those on my personal wish list. There were frisbees, stuffed animals, coloring books, and checkers, but nothing flashy or uniquely special. I had never thought to ask Santa for a new toothbrush or set of pajamas, yet these items were plentiful and were placed in every gift bag of those staying at the mission.

A new perspective hit me in waves as I mingled with the mission families that day. I slowly realized what loss and desperation must feel like and how unfair it was. As my eyes wandered about the room, my gaze locked with one of the mothers and in that moment, her tears of sorrow let me know that she was having similar thoughts, that Santa would not be delivering the packages her children were yearning for. A tapestry of loss unfolded for many that particular Christmas season: lost hopes, dreams, independence, choice, and, above all, self-respect. Varying degrees of pain and disappointment were woven together, catching everyone off guard with overwhelming feelings of despair.

In the aftermath of this experience, I realized the stark difference between hearing about homelessness and loss and witnessing these harsh realities firsthand with my parents. The emotions that unfolded around me, the tangible pain, and the profound impact on the lives of those in the shelter became transformative. It was an experience that changed me, making the struggles and challenges of others more palpable and it placed in me a compelling desire to help others rewrite their life's story.

Understanding Loss:

Embarking into adulthood, my passion for helping others led me into the fields of medicine and human services. Each step, from teaching life skills to managing a clinic for homeless adults, felt like a puzzle piece fitting seamlessly into my life. The echoes of my childhood volunteering at the mission resonated as I directed a shelter program for an international organization.

In this pursuit, I uncovered the diverse facets of loss, that to some degree, impact everyone. Although the experience of any loss is uniquely felt, we see universal responses that are associated with various forms of loss. The death of an elderly parent may seem more manageable as loss unfolds more gradually through the aging process. In contrast, the impact of losing a spouse is often more extreme when the surviving partner is also thrust into different roles of responsibility. Grief is often intensified when there is a substantial reliance on what or who was lost as seen when a young child loses their parent.

When considering loss, one undeniable truth emerges—no one is immune to the profound impact of loss. Whether it is the loss of one's health, stability, or a loved one, everyone faces the reality of losing something or someone they value, challenging the griever to create a new sense of normalcy.

A Story of Support and Empowerment

After years of working with individuals and families grappling with different forms of loss, personal grief, and the intricate process of rebuilding, there is one particular story that stands out—a poignant narrative of resilience, forgiveness, and ultimately, happiness. At the request of those involved, I am respecting their privacy by excluding finer details, yet this heart-wrenching tale illuminates the varying degrees of loss and the transformative journey of a family that weathered a season of trauma.

It was late in the day when a family of five entered my office seeking shelter, each member clutching a black trash bag containing their most cherished possessions. Evicted from their home, their personal belongings had been discarded unceremoniously by their callous landlord. Their arrival marked the inception of a harrowing chapter.

The mother, feeling unwell, was being transported to the emergency room by the father. It was her birthday, and the prospect of her being too ill to celebrate weighed heavily on their three children. Tear-filled eyes exchanged glances as their parents departed, leaving deep feelings of uncertainty.

That ominous afternoon set in motion a chain of events that would forever alter the course of their lives. That fateful night claimed the life of their beloved mother and wife on her birthday.

Struggling to navigate the predictable effects of loss, the father engulfed in shock, found himself incapable of decision-making. Bereft of funds for a funeral and amidst familial discord, he chose to cancel the memorial service. Relieved at not having to attend their mother's funeral, a calmness began to settle on the now family of four.

The ensuing weeks blurred together as the family sought refuge in the shelter's temporary quarters, each member ensnared in their currents of despair. The father, struggling to meet daily needs, found it difficult to focus on his children.

Intervening in a Crisis:

When assisting those experiencing a personal crisis it is essential to remain intentionally observant. Crisis intervention is a helping process that provides a safe space for sufferers to talk through the complexities of their loss, and when tandomed with problem-solving, one's healing can begin. Assisting in decision-making empowers the sufferer, helping them review available options, consequences, and any pros and cons associated with the loss.

The journey through loss is anything but linear; it does not come with a script dictating where to begin and when to pause. Crisis intervention, especially in the stage of immediate turmoil, does not interpret feelings nor does it give direct advice because the focus is placed on emergent care.

Amid a crisis, the power of assurance becomes a lifeline. Efforts extended in crisis intervention assure the sufferer that they are not alone, pledging support whenever they choose to reach out. The goal is to minimize distress, helping those who are suffering to adapt to the disruptions caused by their loss.

Adapting to Loss:

Each child faced the loss of their mother in distinct ways. The two tween sons, inseparable, denied the changed reality, clinging to their daily routines of video games and television. The older brother, unconsciously adopting a caretaker role, contrasted sharply with the demanding nature of his younger brother. Both resisted engaging with other shelter youth, declining every invitation to play. Each response was a unique thread in the complex tapestry of their grief.

Disbelief & Denial:

Our mind's ability to cope relies on responses such as *disbelief and denial* to lessen the initial impact of a loss. This is our body's reaction to a devastating occurrence and is meant to protect us until we are ready to face the reality of the loss.

These responses cushion the blow until we can re-adjust & adapt our thinking to accommodate the sudden change that has taken place.

Disbelief, shock, & denial are normal responses if they are temporary.

A problem occurs when one refuses to face or is unable to accept their loss &/or the reality of their hurt. When this is the case, professional assistance is recommended.

The loss of their mother deeply affected their little sister. She was angry and resistant to any attention. Rejecting acts of kindness, she refused her father's attention. Nightmares disrupted her sleep, intensifying irritability, and her interactions with others grew more boisterous daily. She could not understand why God took her Mommy to heaven, and so her prayers were based on promises that if she would be a good girl, maybe God would bring her back.

Anger or Bargaining:

Often, anger stems from fear. Fear of the unknown can cause doubt, uncertainty, loneliness, etc.

Anger can be directed at ourselves, at the one who died, or at the one who was expected to protect us from hurt and harm.

Bargaining can be a response to wanting a situation to change. For instance, making a promise to change so the loss does not occur. Some resort to bargaining with God to grant relief from the pain or be rescued from a situation.

If the grief is not relieved, over time this can lead to a lifetime of guilt, hurt, condemnation, anger, &/or hatred. When this is the case, professional assistance is also recommended.

The father felt the burdens of his world resting solely on his shoulders as their losses seemed unsurmountable. The loss of his wife and his children's mother, their home, pet, family support, belongings, friends, security, independence, and overall wellness was overwhelming. Whether it's divorce, health problems, or death, grief hits hard and is often weighed down by misery and depression. As though wearing a cloak woven in despair, the family's hopelessness was felt both physically and emotionally.

Supporting this family meant creating a safe space for feelings to flow. Each grief journey is unique, and understanding that, I knew building a connection at the father's pace was key. Relief would only begin to take place when the family felt heard and accepted.

Every grief story is one of a kind, but what is common is the thread of emotion that links us all. No measure or comparison can capture the depth of loss. Knowing how to support someone in their journey can have a profound impact and make a world of difference.

Provided below are some helpful tips when lending a hand to someone downcast and grief-stricken:

Healing is a Succession of Events:

Everyone experiences a loss to varying degrees & we all respond differently based on our personal life story.

There is one commonality when one is wounded; each one experiences degrees of pain & suffering and therefore everyone is subject to varying phases of healing.

Healing is a process that consists of small steps and cannot be rushed. Each step is a forwardward movement and offers comfort as each day, week, month, and year pass.

Attending Behavior:

My main focus for this family was understanding how each person felt internally. This helped me to be more effective when offering support. I used a method referred to as Attending Behavior, which involves listening and displaying genuine care. This simple approach became a key tool in navigating their grief and helping each member experience positive changes.

The hallmark characteristics of Attending Behavior require proficiency to be effective and include such methods as:

Verbal Following: direct or subtle communication to encourage and promote positive interaction.

Vocal Style: the use of volume, pace, and pitch of voice to affirm, soothe, and express sincerity.

Facial Expressions: remaining mindful of eyebrows, eyes, and mouth as they are micro-expressions that convey information.

Body Language: consists of nonverbal indicators that relay conscious and unconscious messages that either align or contradict what is being verbalized.

While acutely listening to the father's story, he opened up about the prejudices he faced throughout his life — childhood bullying, mistreatment from neighbors, job rejections, and difficulties finding housing. These painful experiences tinted how he saw his life. Given the lingering impact of these oppressions, it was understandable that he hesitated to share openly, leaving him feeling discouraged and distrustful.

GUIDANCE FOR THE HELPER:

In my years of providing aid to those in need, I have learned that genuine help is most effective when offered with a true intention to assist. Building a foundation of care and concern takes time but is essential in establishing trust.

By taking this approach, the family began to feel understood, fostering a sense of connection. While communication styles varied among family members, they all realized that their well-being was of the utmost importance.

The father, at times, preferred shorter conversations, while at other times he welcomed longer visits. In every instance, I remained genuinely interested without intruding. Transparency was somewhat challenging for him. He struggled to share his loss and how it would affect his family's future. The weight of new responsibilities, finding employment, securing affordable housing, and facing limited prospects overwhelmed him with anxiety.

Active Listening:

To be a proficient helper, one must break free from one's personal perspectives as well as mindsets to effectively connect with those seeking assistance. Genuine respect is built through active listening, which encourages understanding and acknowledges feelings. This skill replaces fixed points of view with positive viewpoints, fostering respect and satisfaction in relationships.

Active listening requires the helper's intentional focus, especially when immediate needs are emergent. It is essential to create a comfortable space for sufferers to disclose their feelings and needs and active listening sends the message that you are hearing what is both said and not said.

It is a popular thought that the fear of the unknown is the greatest fear of all. And the loss of someone or something valued can seem overwhelmingly uncertain. Knowing that fear is an underlying emotion often linked to anger assures the helper not to take the client's blunt or negative responses personally - as the helper is also a sounding board for those experiencing a crisis.

Rephrasing what is heard provides comfort and assurance to the sufferer, as this technique validates the sufferer's feelings. Statements such as, "I hear your concerns. You've experienced a lot of loss, and you're wondering what to do next." helps to affirm the surferer's experience without committing oneself.

Engaging with the father on this level of communication helped him understand that his feelings of frustration and anger were normal reactions to his distress. Paraphrasing, assessing the family's needs, and reducing confusion, all improved the father's efforts. Active listening became a foundation for addressing the family's losses. This approach enabled the father to recognize old mindsets as he considered embracing new growth-centered views, which resulted in creating new possibilities for the family.

PROBLEM SOLVING; THROUGH EMPOWERMENT AND CRITICAL THINKING:

Helping the sufferer define their loss leads to understanding their capabilities. Active listening during crisis intervention encourages conversations that offer emotional support as uncertainties unfold.

After reflecting, the father acknowledged that despite his wife's chronic illness, he had strongly depended on his wife as the family's primary caregiver. He relied not only on her income but also on her household management skills. Now, with these responsibilities solely on his shoulders, he felt utterly alone in his depth of despair. This is where true problem-solving becomes a tool for empowerment and critical thinking.

As bystanders, we can miss the fact that when someone is in the midst of turmoil they often cannot break down a solution into steps. For those offering assistance, it is helpful to aid the sufferer by breaking down challenges into manageable steps that foster progress. Brainstorming explores solutions and alternatives, creating coping strategies that distinguish between crucial and inconsequential aspects of one's loss.

The following problem-solving steps helped this now single father of three as he tried to cope with the varied phases of his loss:

PROBLEM SOLVING STEP 1: Building Trust; A Journey of Connection

When someone is facing a major loss, seeking comfort from others can be both difficult and challenging. Feelings can seem too personal, leading to such thoughts as, "What if they don't understand?" or "What if they judge me?" Overcoming these hurdles was crucial for this father and his family, and it was plain to see that establishing a level of trust was necessary before moving on.

To bridge this invisible gap, I took intentional steps to show my commitment to each family member. Recognizing their feelings of social exclusion, I understood that their progress hinged on building trust. Reflecting on their individual experiences, I avoided assumptions, allowing the family to feel understood.

While creating a warm and inviting environment for meaningful interactions, I spent time with the family which helped me understand their qualities. Observing their behaviors, I knew when to speak and when to remain silent, ensuring my interactions were empathetic.

Communication, trust, and respect are vital in any relationship, especially when dealing with complex challenges. Years of assisting people with various issues underscored the importance of making individuals feel appreciated and respected. This approach of validating the father's feelings while actively listening to his concerns, encouraged him to remain engaged as we addressed how each one impacted the welfare of his family's future.

Remaining consistently engaged establishes authentic relationships. By doing so, I positively influenced how the father and his children perceived the acceptance of help. Although building these genuine connections took time, the association between respect and trust naturally improved the quality of this family's care.

PROBLEM-SOLVING STEP 2: Person-Centered Care; Focusing on Wellness and Basic Needs

Understanding that relationships are key to person-centered care, the focus shifted to the family's wellness, health, values, goals, dreams, and wishes. In each meeting, I became the father's personal team member, supporting him as he confronted the depth of his loss.

Starting with the family's basic needs as individuals, and not as just a single unit, was crucial. Emphasizing self-care, I reminded the father that it is a vital part of the healing process. This person-centered approach aimed to address their daily functions and individual well-being, creating a holistic foundation for their journey through grief.

Creating a Plan for Self-Care:

The helper can positively impact the wellness of the sufferer by gently reminding them to include self-care in their daily routine.

Self-care eases one's suffering as it offers relief to one's mind, spirit, and body.

Getting plenty of sleep before an event or daily demand - helps with resiliency.

The helper can offer suggestions such as, "Maybe attending only a portion of the event, rather than in its entirety would be more manageable for you."

The helper can recommend to the sufferer to attend the event accompanied by a loved one, so they have someone to lean on.

The helper can suggest to the sufferer to arrange their transportation, so they are free to make last-minute changes if necessary.

The helper can encourage the sufferer to have some ready-made responses stored away in their mind, so they are not caught off guard or feel awkward: "I am doing as well as expected, thank you for your concern."

PROBLEM SOLVING STEP 3: Building Bonds; Transforming Loss into Hope

Establishing routines brought a positive shift, making the family more receptive to engagement. Recognizing the importance of parental consent, I focused on connecting with the father's children. While the boys welcomed my attention, the little sister initially hesitated.

Focusing on shared interests, we played games, read books, and took walks. Icebreakers helped find common ground, and soon, the boys included me in their playtime. The brothers craved my attention as if replacing something lost – someone's undivided focus. In just a few encounters, our relationship turned into a genuine friendship.

As interactions unfolded, the little sister's curiosity grew, and she soon joined in, snuggling into my arms as her brothers played. The invisible wall around the children started to crumble, which resulted in the father becoming more interactive as well.

Considering the family's history of feeling let down, trust was crucial for their progress and had to be rebuilt over time. Years of unpredictable environments had instilled attitudes that no one cared. Helping the father recognize and change these fixed mindsets became a primary focus in this family's self-care.

PROBLEM SOLVING STEP 4: Changing Mindsets; From Hopelessness to Growth

Mindsets, shaped by experiences, can be either adaptive or maladaptive. The father had developed a fixed mindset, convinced of an unchangeable and hopeless fate. Our visits encouraged him to reflect on these long-term patterns, and then identify and adjust any negative mindsets that were formed through past negative experiences.

Acknowledging that his negative thoughts hindered his self-confidence, the father traced them back to childhood criticism. Changing these ingrained mindsets required determination and hard work; understanding the "why" and "what" behind his preformed thoughts paved the way for forming new perspectives and pursuing new dreams and goals.

The journey toward transformational change began with the father embracing new opportunities and looking forward to a positive future.

PROBLEM-SOLVING STEP 5: Understanding Exhaustion and Mental Fatigue

Coming to an understanding that grief-induced mental and physical exhaustion were normal side effects caused by loss, the father learned that sorrow can alter one's memory and ability to reason. Therefore, it is essential to be mindful that when one is in the depth of loss, their capacity to handle added stress can feel overwhelming.

It is very helpful to remain aware of one's mental health. This helps discern if the individual feels equipped to handle the degree of strife caused by the loss. If not, then professional help is recommended.

Concentrating on what one values offers some degree of distraction. This practice helps to shift one's focus from hopelessness to one of hopefulness. Although initially, the results are short-term, over time, this approach offers extended periods of relief.

Meditating on positive outcomes and reflecting on areas of importance are positive forms of mindfulness and these are healthy distractions.

In time, the sufferer will feel able to reflect on positive memories and this helps with soothing one's pain.

PROBLEM SOLVING STEP 6: Navigating Grief; From Pain to Healing

Both loss and death are a universal reality of life. We find ourselves wrestling with a profound sense of injustice when faced with the unfairness of losing someone or something we hold dear. Pain, agony, fear, guilt, and helplessness became companions on this family's unwelcome journey. Their emotions, unique to each family member, manifested externally as mourning—a crucial part of bereavement.

Although mourning is felt internally and often guided by personal beliefs, it is expressed externally. Mourning is a healing process that begins when loss is demonstrated outwardly. Some traditions encourage wearing all black, some hold memorial services, and some demonstrate their grief through public wailing or weeping. For this family, such displays were viewed as weaknesses.

The father, facing multi-layered pain, initially tried to postpone facing the reality of their loss. Canceling his wife's funeral was an unintended interruption to the family's mourning process. It was driven by the mindset of being weak and also his desire to shield them all from the harsh reality of their loved one's death. However, avoidance only delayed this family's ability to reconcile their loss.

Although the father made a concerted effort to avoid any displays of emotion, his children were emotionally exhausted from trying to mimic his behavior. Once the father discovered the importance of allowing both himself and his children to grieve outwardly, he began to see each one step out and away from their all-consuming pain and into a place of healing.

PROBLEM-SOLVING STEP 7: Guilt & Shame

The weight and burden of loss can make existing day by day feel like a daunting task. Sufferers often consumed by guilt and shame, struggle to cope. Extensions of guilt can surface as sufferers anticipate the impact of the loss on others, leading to a downcast feeling when needs go unmet. This was certainly the case for members of this family. The father felt guilty that his children had lost their mother, and the children felt responsible for her illness as they wondered if they were to blame.

Commonly, grief and guilt run parallel with one another. Some sufferers hold themselves responsible for the loss and carrying this burden can interfere with the grieving process.

Feelings of blame and guilt are commonly expressed through self-recrimination. This self-blame is often associated with such thoughts as, "I should have done something to help." or "It is my fault, I didn't see what was happening." Holding oneself responsible for perceived shortcomings can heighten one's burden of guilt and this degree of regret extends one's grieving process.

Once this family worked through the phases of their wife and mother's chronic illness, they eventually came to terms with the fact that they were not responsible for her passing, and their feelings of regret, shame, and guilt, began to lighten over time.

PROBLEM SOLVING STEP 8: Experiencing Grief:

Grieving has no set timeline, and its impact varies. Understanding grief's emotional toll provided this father some relief. Explaining that feelings evolve and that they can encompass shock, sadness, anger, and guilt, helped the father process his thoughts.

As the father worked through the different phases of grief, he came to realize that some factors are beyond one's control and this fact offered relief from his nagging feelings of regret and helplessness. Over time, the family's need for clear answers diminished, and their acceptance that not every outcome can be explained, began to pave the way for reconciliation.

Realizing that mourning was essential, the father organized a service in his wife's memory. Contrary to his belief that no one cared, the community showed their support through donations that covered funeral costs. A graveside service provided closure, as the children attached their love notes to balloons and watched them ascend toward heaven to deliver their unspoken messages to their mother.

It was reassuring to each member that they were where they belonged. As community members showed their support to each one, the family began to feel accepted. This helped immensely as each one began to feel their sense of value and belonging restored, replacing their pervasive sadness with newfound hope.

UNDERSTANDING COMMON SIDE EFFECTS OF GRIEF:

By better understanding the grieving process, individuals are better equipped to face day-to-day challenges. When one knows what to expect, it provides a degree of solace. This was certainly the case for this father. He discovered a sense of relief once he was helped in identifying healthy responses to grief. Having clarity removes uncertainty and confusion and helps guide individuals through the phases of healing. Knowledge restores hope and wellness to those suffering and in this father's case, knowing what to expect, empowered him on his journey toward healing.

The side effects from grief can linger as the jolt from such intense emotion impacts one's life in other areas. Being well-informed is helpful to those who wonder what the future holds as they try to move forward.

Physical Responses to Grief

Over time, it became apparent that the depth of grief this family was experiencing placed a physical toll on their overall health. The father experienced increased headaches, the daughter struggled with sleep and tummy aches, and the sons faced joy-stealing challenges. Thankfully, professional intervention provided relief.

Learning how to cope, each family member was introduced to emotion-based coping skills that they learned to turn to when feeling overwhelmed. They gladly adopted self-care routines. Encouraged to be physically active and how to practice mindfulness, they began to find relief from their grief-related symptoms. Each one applied effort in their areas of interest. The sister enjoyed coloring, the brothers listened to music - each their own genre, and the father found relief through physical exercise, which proved effective in reducing his stress.

Spiritual Responses to Grief

The family, practicing self-care, rediscovered comfort in their faith. Despite initial feelings of God letting them down, they sought meaning and understanding. The father, leaning into his faith, sought a deeper sense of belonging and hope. Reinforcing a Christian perspective, he assured his children of their mother's eternal life, finding peace and hope as they relied on their spiritual community for comfort.

It is helpful to know that although spiritual communities and practices offer a sense of connection and support, it is not always easy for someone who has relied on their faith to turn to their church community for comfort. This is because those who have committed their lives to God, often struggle to reconcile that they still feel vulnerable when facing adversities. This is a common and normal response. Feeling disappointed and let down by God, some turn away from seeking Him for comfort. Processing this form of grief takes time, and those offering support should be patient, steadfast, and filled with love because, for a time, there can be a degree of discomfort in places of worship.

Socializing as it Relates to Grief:

Those experiencing grief often resist socializing because it can demand a level of energy that requires extended interactions as well as personal explanations. When one is in the grip of grief, one finds it requires a great deal of effort to stay present and in the moment of daily interactions. When one's soul is damaged and one's heart is broken, these emotional injuries can cause one to feel emotionally depleted.

It is helpful to know that human connections are vital for wellness. Face-to-face contact restores the present moment, shifts perspectives, and introduces new possibilities for restoring hope. As a helper, this is one way to support the sufferer as they begin to mend. Through encouragement, helpers can make suggestions, extend invitations, and accompany the suffering to events all while shedding new light on untraveled paths that offer new prospects and promise.

For this family of four, the shelter's support group provided relief. The children formed new friendships, and the father connected with other single parents which provided him some insight that there was light at the end of his grief-filled tunnel. In just a matter of weeks, the family considered the support of this group an extension of good friends that offered continued fellowship.

Embracing Change After Grief; Creating New Traditions

Maintaining routines can be both difficult and challenging. This is because memories of a lost loved one are enhanced when it becomes apparent that their absence is permanent. It is very helpful to encourage the sufferer to consider creating new traditions. Changing routines opens up new possibilities and adds an element of newness as sufferers work through the healing process. Although allowing each member to move forward at their own pace is helpful, it is good to keep in mind that trying something new can create a sense of peace and newfound joy.

This family discovered that changing some of their family traditions made it easier for them to cope through the holidays. Instead of celebrating Thanksgiving with a traditional turkey dinner, they enjoyed a buffet with other shelter families that was provided by a local restaurant. By no longer having their artificial Christmas tree, they were provided with an opportunity to hike through a tree farm and cut down their own tree. These are just a couple of ways this family began to create new traditions that led to new experiences and precious memories.

The Season of Relief:

As the family progressed, their grief journey led to rebuilding their life as they transitioned into gradual acceptance. Settling into "Pressing On," they focused on the future, unburdened by their earlier feelings of despair.

The family began to take an ***Upward Turn:*** This is when anguish and pain gradually wane, paving the way for a serene and relaxed state of mind.

The family eventually looked forward to ***Rebuilding & Renewal:*** The fractures caused by their loss began to heal, with life's pieces finding their places. The prospect of moving forward started to feel tangible.

The family transitioned into feelings of ***Acceptance & Hope*:** This is when one slowly begins to accept their new reality - which brings forth feelings of hope, hinting at a restored future.

As days melted into weeks and weeks into months, the father envisioned once-deemed unattainable dreams now within his reach. Recognizing the array of choices available to his family, he shifted from accepting the bare minimum to setting achievable goals.

His yearning to reclaim ownership of his life transformed from a distant desire to a palpable reality. What once seemed unrealistic now felt achievable, and he was resolute in discarding past mindsets that in past years had hindered the progress of his family's future.

Embracing this positive approach of recognizing patterns of thoughts and behaviors, the father began prioritizing his goals, hopes, and dreams. He became intentional when contemplating the ideal living situation, finding suitable work that offered flexibility for single parenting, and even saw the benefit of mending family bonds. Despite confronting some lost pride, the father deemed this hard work as being worthwhile for the sake of his family's overall welfare.

Fading Bereavement and a New Beginning:

This family's personal journey manifests the power of resilience, self-care, and community support in overcoming the most challenging circumstances. The family's progress was not without struggles and distress, but their unwavering belief in creating a new future strengthened their entire family unit.

Their inspiring tale stands as a testament to the profound strength of the human spirit and its ability to transcend even the most profound loss. By harnessing communal ties, pursuing self-improvement, and finding solace in spiritual beliefs, they turned their tragedy into hope and their despair into purpose.

Today, the father proudly asserts that he and his family are genuinely happy, attributing their progress to a supportive program that provided transitional housing and case management. His determination to break generational patterns fueled positive change, which led to his securing an associate degree and a supervisory role in landscaping. In his desire to give back, the father established a community garden on the shelter property that, to this day, is a haven for healing.

This family's experience serves as a reminder that, in the face of tragedy, it is possible to find comfort in rebuilding and embracing life with renewed vigor and optimism. As their narrative continues to unfold, the family looks forward to the future with a steadfast resolve. In rewriting their story, the family has proven that even the deepest scars can heal, and new beginnings can flourish.

HELPFUL TIPS FOR THE HELPER:

Mistaken Views: It is common to have preset views and to reflect them onto others. For instance, an opinion of how one should grieve a loss or how long one's mourning should be practiced. Provided below are common expressions that are best avoided:

Believing that what was lost can be replaced or substituted with something better.

Believing that grief & mourning are similar & occur in predictable stages.

Believing that feelings of grief should be avoided & gotten over quickly.

Believing that being upset is a sign of weakness (in one's faith also).

Believing that when someone dies, we only miss them physically.

Believing that grief & feelings of loss eventually go away for good.

Believing that It helps to avoid thinking of the loss during holidays & special events.

When offering support, it is helpful for the helper to be present in the sufferer's pain. This means remaining available to listen and offer encouragement. Resist taking on the responsibility of trying to heal or replace others with yourself. Strive to accept & respect this time of uncertainty and not impose order or logic onto the sufferer.

It reflects empathy when you listen with your heart and not with your head. Try not to determine how someone should feel or heal. Remain supportive. Avoiding judgments & steer away from giving advice or direction unless asked.

It is helpful to know that stillness is valued by those who are bereaved. Filling in the silence(s) can feel overwhelming for all parties. There is no need to talk or entertain, just be present.

Helpful Acts For Those Who Want to Help:

Remain in touch often. Send cards on holidays & at special times - include a note. Mention the name of the lost one, reflect on their wonderful qualities, or refer to the sad event while offering support

Arrange assistance for meals, run errands, help with tasks, babysit, etc.

Ask, Ask, Ask...do not give up extending invitations. Offers remind the sufferer that they are special and missed. It is common to distance oneself from those who are mourning, but this is precisely when they need support. Regular invitations offer solace and joy to the life of the sufferer. Be persistent.

Be conscious that attending events alone can cause some discomfort to the sufferer. Offering to share a ride, sit with them, or include other singles is very helpful when arranging or attending an event.

Speak Words Carefully:

It is helpful to know that the sufferer may be personally sensitive to words or phrases that seem offensive. Often, statements made by well-intentioned people can contribute to personal or spiritual distress. Provided below are common statements made that are best avoided as they can feel hurtful. Statements that are associated with one's walk in faith can deepen one's anguish, anger &/or rejection of God :

God needed him in heaven.

Everything happens for a reason.

Heaven needed another angel.

God will never give you more than you can handle.

Positive Expressions of Concern: The following are examples of well-received verbalized offers of support:

"I am sorry for your pain. How can I help you?"

"I have no idea what you are going through, but I am here to lean on at any time."

"I am here for you and want to offer you my support."

"Don't feel like you have to be strong for me, just know that I am here for you."

"Do not feel embarrassed, your reaction is normal. "

"If you would ever would like to talk about what happened, I am here to support you."

SELF-HELP TIPS FOR THE SUFFERER:

Holiday Self-Care Plan; A Season of Healing:

Begin by considering how you do or do not want to celebrate a particular holiday.

Ask yourself if there are traditions or rituals associated with a holiday that you feel are important to maintain.

Do you feel that some can be altered – at least for this immediate season?

Take time to identify what is most important to you and try to organize your plans around these preferences or valued principles.

It is not uncommon to dread special events or holidays after experiencing a loss. Many wish to avoid attending because of vivid reminders of what has been lost &/or what will be missed.

You may not be able to control WHEN an occasion takes place, but you do have control over HOW to experience it.

Being prepared offers significant relief. Having a plan lessens one's fear, anxiety, & feelings of vulnerability.

Being prudent (being cautious or showing care for the future) is therapeutic & offers a place of refuge as healing takes place.

Being Proactive is a Positive Approach:

Think through any past &/or current challenges with people or circumstances and decide what you are or are not able to face currently.

Could communicating beforehand alleviate the forth-coming awkwardness or discomfort that may come from an in-person encounter? Such as, "I will not be attending this year's event, but hope to feel up to it in the future."

Putting a plan in place for the occasional "what ifs" can offer you a degree of peace and self-confidence. By having a plan, you provide yourself a way out if one is needed. For instance:

If you are too tired to attend: Notify others that you are too tired.

If you are overwhelmed with grief: Make your excuses beforehand so that you can lessen any anxiety. This also allows you to make other plans that offer you relief (which also provides you with a reason why you are not able to do something).

If someone hurts or offends you at an event: be prepared...this will very likely happen. When one is in the depths of despair, they are often tender and sensitive and even the most innocent words and actions can feel hurtful. Should this take place, having a pat response will assist you as you try to cope with the situation. A clear and concise statement such as, " I am unable to talk about that right now. I may feel up to it at another time - I will let you know." can be helpful.

Take Care of You!

Make certain to acknowledge & express your feelings as you experience them. This helps in processing loss and identifying where your focus is placed. This will help to recognize specific areas that need attention and will help guide you when or if you choose to seek professional help with coping with the feelings of loss.

Sharing your story can be very healing. This process helps align your heart with your head which can be very powerful as you face the outcome(s) of your loss. Avoid self-criticism when you feel the need to talk about your pain. This is a normal process of mourning and is very comforting - so surround yourself with those who encourage and support you as you work through this phase. Keep in mind that grief support groups are a safe place to ruminate (telling your story) and it is often comforting to be in the company of others who are also grieving.

Try to manage your stress daily. Lighten your schedule, and lessen your demands until you are better able to handle more. Keep in mind that stress is more manageable when you get enough sleep, nutrition, and exercise.

Regularly prioritize & reset your expectations. Begin with small things first and then move on to those that are more demanding. For instance, write a few thank you cards at a time, rather than trying to get them all in the mail on the same day.

Set new routines for applying self-care. Be patient with yourself. It takes time to reestablish a new way to live life but once you find what is satisfying to you, this will bring you comfort.

Holding on to a personal object(s) that reminds you of your loved-one can provide a level of comfort for a time. Such objects as clothing, photos, a prized possession can help you feel close to the one you miss. At some point in your healing, you may find that you no longer need to hold on to the item and may choose to keep the item as a keepsake or give it away as you feel more reconciled over time. Keep in mind that discarding a loved one's items does not equate with one's level of grief as there are those that believe it is just too painful to have constant reminders of their loss. Although momentos can be helpful at different points in time and during varying seasons of life, be careful not to create a shrine (when someone maintains/creates a space just as it was before the death) as this can hinder one's ability to move beyond the reality that their loved one has died.

Remain open to trying new things. Include fresh views and different perspectives in your decision-making. Do not be afraid to meet new people, try new things, or go to new places as these attempts in restoring your joy will become fulfilling as you choose to live intentionally.

And Finally, Be Well With Your Soul!

Treasure what was good & have that be a driving force that keeps you strong as you move forward.

Do not lose hope – be assured that with each new season comes another phase of healing.

Allow your soul to find peace in knowing that although life may now look differently, your life's story continues on and will include new found joy!

Chapter Four

The Journey to Self-Love: Becoming Your Own Best Friend

By Joelle Rabow Maletis MAED, MA, LMFT

A trauma-informed therapist who teaches people how to rebuild their lives with self-love and resilience.

For years I believed I was strong because I kept going. I believed I was disciplined because I pushed myself harder than anyone around me. I believed I was fine because I did not stop long enough to feel anything. I built an identity on survival, not knowing that survival is not the same as living.

My first experience with real grief came when the career I had built my life around ended overnight. One day I was a professional dancer, and the next I was told my body could no longer do what I had trained it to do since childhood. The world I lived in did not prepare me for what came next. I had sacrificed so much for that dream. I had lost sleep, celebrations, relationships, and time I could never get back. Nothing prepares you for the moment when the future you built your identity on simply disappears.

When injuries hit, I slipped into a deep sadness. I mourned the version of myself I believed I would become. I mourned the structure, the pride, the recognition. I mourned the dream that shaped my entire childhood and adulthood. When people experience this kind of loss, they often assume they should bounce back quickly, but the truth is that losing a dream is losing a part of yourself. I did not know how to process that loss, so I kept moving forward in the only way I knew how.

Life continued to unravel until it became impossible to ignore. I found myself thirty four years old, in a collapsing marriage, raising two small children, caught in postpartum depression, wrestling with infant loss, and living with PTSD. I kept thinking that if I worked a little harder or held myself together a little longer, everything would fix itself. I was still using survival as a strategy long after survival was no longer enough.

When your life blows up, you discover the places you have been avoiding. And I had been avoiding myself for a long time.

The day I finally went to therapy, it was not because I recognized my own pain. It was because I wanted to fix my marriage. I thought therapy was something you did to save relationships, not something you did to save yourself. I did not walk in expecting to change my life. I walked in hoping to change someone else.

In reality, I needed therapy.

I had experienced trauma that I never named because I did not think I was allowed to. I was carrying grief in my mind and body that I treated like a personal flaw instead of a wound. When you grow up believing that value comes from endurance, you learn to ignore every sign of burnout until your body, your relationships, and your life collapse.

My therapist changed everything. She saw the truth in me before I could. She did not see weakness where I saw failure. She did not see brokenness where I saw shame. She saw a woman who had survived more than she realized. She saw someone who needed a safe place to fall apart so she could learn how to build something new.

That was the first moment I experienced real self love.

Self love is not a feeling of confidence. It is not a perfect morning routine. It is not about pretending you are okay. Self love begins the moment you allow yourself to be seen. When you stop performing strength and start admitting you are hurting, the healing begins. Self love starts with honesty.

I remember many nights where I tucked my children into bed, cleaned the kitchen, and then stayed up studying until three in the morning. I woke up a few hours later, packed lunches, drove them to school, and pushed through my day as if nothing was wrong. That is what survival looks like. You learn to perform wellness even when you are falling apart.

Self love taught me I did not have to live like that.

Therapy gave me skills I did not know I needed. I learned how to ground myself when my mind raced. I learned how to breathe instead of panic. I learned how to recognize thoughts that were hurting me. I learned how to give myself grace when old perfectionistic patterns resurfaced. I learned that I did not need to be flawless to be worthy. I learned that setbacks did not mean I was failing.

Self love is not something you master once. It is something that ebbs and flows. It is something you practice, forget, return to, and try again. There are still mornings when I wake up and think I am still a dancer because my muscles ache the same way they used to. There are still moments where the old pressure to be perfect tries to return. But the difference now is that I know how to love myself through it.

I learned that being imperfect does not make me unlovable. It makes me human.

My identity had always been wrapped in being a ballerina; the performance. In dance I wore a mask on stage. In life I wore the mask of achievement. Therapy asked me to take the mask off. It asked me to stop hiding behind roles. It asked me to be vulnerable.

Ironically, becoming a therapist allowed me to hide again, but in a healthier way. My work is not about me. I become a conduit. I become a safe place for others. I hold their stories, their pain, and their healing. In dance I hid behind characters. In therapy I support others behind the scenes. Both allow me to step aside, but only one allows me to help someone change their life.

And that is where my love for this work was born.

If I had a magic wand, I would give everyone the gift of self love. But if self love were easy, therapists would not exist. It is one thing to explain how to ground yourself. It is another thing to actually do it when you are anxious. It is easy to teach someone to visualize a stop sign, breathe, and ask what they need. It is much harder to do those things yourself when fear is loud.

But self love is not about perfection. Self love is about practice.

The most powerful lesson I learned is that self love is not the absence of mistakes or flaws. It is the presence of grace.

Self love tells you that even when life collapses, you can rebuild. Even when dreams die, you can dream again. Even when you feel lost, you are still worthy of love. Even when you do not know where to go next, you can take one small step.

That choice — that moment of self love — led me to the career I adore today.

I never imagined loving something as much as I loved dancing, but being a therapist gave me a new purpose. Helping people heal, teaching them the skills I wish I had earlier, and giving them what I never had for myself — that is self love in action.

I do not wish the injuries away. I do not wish the pain away. I do not wish the grief away. Those experiences led me to the life I love. They shaped me into someone who can help others find their way out of their own darkness. If I could go through it all again, I would, because it gave me my life's work.

And now I know this:

I am the sum of all my experiences, good, bad, and indifferent.
I am perfectly imperfect.
And so are you.

Self love is not the end of the story. It is the beginning.

What Self Love Actually Means

When people first hear the phrase self love, they often picture bubble baths, vacations, or a polished morning routine with green juice and soft music. Those things can support your well-being, but they are not the core of self love. Real self love is much harder and much deeper. It asks you to look at the parts of yourself you ignore. It asks you to face the fears you have avoided. It asks you to take responsibility for what you can control and release what you cannot.

Self love is not a mood. It is a choice.

My entire life was built on the belief that love had to be earned through performance. Be perfect. Be disciplined. Be strong. Be quiet. Be helpful. Be small. Be productive. I had earned praise through my achievements and my pain tolerance. I believed if I stopped moving, I would stop mattering. That mindset followed me into adulthood. I pushed through exhaustion, ignored my own needs, and punished myself for not being enough.

The truth is that many of us are taught to love everyone except ourselves. We are taught to give and give until there is nothing left. We are taught to be polite, agreeable, hardworking, and self sacrificing. We are taught that wanting more makes us selfish. We are taught to silence our inner voice and listen to everyone else.

So when the idea of self love appears, it feels uncomfortable.

When I finally started therapy, the hardest part was slowing down long enough to hear my own thoughts. I did not know what I needed because I had spent years avoiding myself. Avoidance is one of the most common coping strategies people use. You stay busy, distracted, overbooked, or emotionally numb. You convince yourself you do not have time to feel anything. Avoidance feels productive, but it only delays healing. What you avoid grows louder. What you refuse to face gains power.

Self love breaks the cycle of avoidance. It invites you to stop running.

I used to think self love would make me weak. I thought slowing down meant losing my edge. I thought being gentle with myself meant giving up. But the more I learned, the more I realized how wrong that belief was.

Self love is strength.

Self love is discipline.

Self love is courage.

Self love is honesty.

Self love is the foundation of growth.

When you learn to love yourself, everything else changes. Your relationships shift. Your goals shift. The people you allow in your life shift. Your sense of worth shifts. You stop chasing validation and start choosing values. You stop shrinking yourself and start showing up in your life.

Self love teaches you to pivot when life demands it.

For a long time, pivoting was something I viewed as failure. I grew up in a time where success meant staying in the same job for thirty years until you retired. Changing paths was seen as unstable or unfocused. Women especially were told that the older we got, the less valuable we became. We were either too old, too tired, too emotional, too busy raising children, too focused on career, too much or not enough. And in society's eyes, aging made us less relevant, not more wise.

But the truth is that pivoting is a skill. Pivoting is resilience. Pivoting is intelligence. Pivoting is self respect.

My life has been a series of pivots. Some were chosen. Some were forced. Every pivot required self love.

Leaving the professional dance world was the first major pivot. Facing the collapse of my marriage pushed me into another. Returning to graduate school again brought me to another. Facing loss, learning trauma theory, raising children alone, building my practice, meeting clients every day who trusted me with their deepest pain—every step required me to ask myself, Who am I allowed to become now?

Self love answers that question.

Self love gives you permission to redefine your identity.

Self love gives you permission to evolve.

Self love gives you permission to try again.

Self love gives you permission to grow even when others doubt you.

Self love gives you permission to choose yourself without guilt.

When I started working with clients, I noticed something universal. Most people had never been taught how to love themselves. They had been taught how to work, how to please, how to endure, how to function, how to fix others, how to perform well, how to avoid conflict, and how to hide their pain. But no one had taught them how to be gentle with themselves. No one had taught them how to sit with hard emotions. No one had taught them how to talk to themselves with kindness. No one had taught them how to accept imperfection.

Self love is not natural for most people. It is learned.

That is why the tools in my workbook focus on simple steps. Identify. Challenge. Replace. These are the foundations of self compassion. You begin by noticing what you feel and what you believe. Then you challenge the beliefs that hurt you. Then you replace them with something supportive. You learn how to reconnect with your body. You learn how to slow your breathing. You learn how to pause instead of react. You learn how to speak to yourself the way you would speak to a child who needs comfort.

It sounds simple, but simple does not mean easy.

Self love takes practice, and practice takes time. You cannot muscle your way into healing. You cannot shame yourself into growth. You cannot criticize yourself into confidence. You cannot push yourself into wholeness. Healing happens through softness and consistency.

Self love is the process of becoming your own safe place.

It is the moment you choose rest instead of punishment.

It is the moment you choose honesty instead of avoidance.

It is the moment you choose boundaries instead of resentment.

It is the moment you choose truth instead of performance.

It is the moment you choose healing instead of self destruction.

The moment I understood this, my life changed. Not overnight. Not instantly. But slowly, day by day. I began noticing when old patterns tried to pull me back. I learned to pause instead of react. I learned that setbacks were not proof of failure but signs that something needed attention. I learned to ask myself, What do I need right now? Sometimes the answer was rest. Sometimes it was courage. Sometimes it was silence. Sometimes it was connection.

Self love is the practice of listening to yourself.

It is not about getting it perfect. It is about showing up for yourself every day even when you feel unworthy. It is about forgiving yourself for not knowing what you know now. It is about accepting that healing is not linear. It is about making space for both joy and pain. It is about recognizing that you are not broken. You are becoming.

Self love is the beginning of the life you actually deserve.

Practicing Self Love in Daily Life

Self love becomes powerful when it leaves your mind and enters your daily life. It is not something you practice once a week or only when you feel good. It is a way of living. It becomes part of how you make decisions, how you speak, how you set boundaries, how you rest, how you recover, and how you build your future.

My life did not change because I understood self love in theory. It changed because I learned how to practice it in real time.

In the beginning, the simplest tools felt impossible. When my therapist first asked me to pause and breathe instead of spiraling, I laughed. I had spent years outrunning my emotions. Slowing down felt dangerous. Stillness felt foreign. Breathing felt like surrender. But she taught me something I never forgot. She said, "You cannot heal what you refuse to feel."

I carried that lesson with me.

Self love means giving yourself permission to feel without judging yourself.

Many people say they want to heal, but they do not want to feel uncomfortable. They want change without vulnerability. They want growth without discomfort. They want healing without honesty. But healing requires truth. The truth of what hurt you. The truth of what you need. The truth of what you avoid. The truth of what you tell yourself when you are alone.

Self love begins with telling the truth to yourself.

When I was going through divorce, postpartum depression, and trauma, my truth was this: I was overwhelmed, grieving, exhausted, lonely, scared, and trying to keep everything together for everyone else. I had never said those words out loud until therapy. Saying the truth gave me back my power. Avoidance had taken it. Honesty returned it.

Once you tell the truth, you can begin to repair.

One of the most important skills in self love is the ability to pause. People underestimate how life changing a pause can be. Your pause interrupts automatic patterns. It creates space. It slows the spiral. It lets your nervous system settle. It gives you a chance to respond instead of react.

In my workbook, I teach the Identify, Challenge, and Replace technique. These steps were born from both neuroscience, empirical theory and personal experience. They are the foundation of rewiring your mind.

Identify is the moment you pause and notice what is happening inside you.

Challenge is the moment you question whether your thoughts are true or helpful.

Replace is the moment you choose a different response.

These steps create new patterns. They slowly undo the harmful stories you have repeated to yourself for years.

For example, in my own life, the moment I felt overwhelmed, my mind used to say, "You are failing." The moment I rested, my mind said, "You are falling behind." The moment I could not keep up, my mind said, "You are not enough." I believed these thoughts because they were familiar. But familiar does not mean true.

Self love teaches you to challenge the beliefs that hurt you.

When I learned to challenge my thoughts, everything softened. Instead of "You are failing," I learned to replace it with, "You are allowed to be tired." Instead of "You are behind," I replaced it with, "You are doing your best with what you have." Instead of "You are not enough," I replaced it with, "You are worthy as you are."

These simple shifts changed the way I lived.

Self love is not one big transformation. It is a thousand small choices made over and over again.

I saw these changes in my clients too. I watched people walk into my office ashamed, overwhelmed, or convinced that something was wrong with them. I watched them unravel the beliefs that had been placed on them. I watched them learn how to ask for help, how to say no, how to speak up, how to set boundaries, how to rest without guilt, and how to build a life that felt like their own.

Self love becomes real when you practice it in the moments that matter.

When your mind goes quiet at night and the old thoughts return.
When someone is disappointed in you and you feel the urge to shrink.
When you take a step toward something new and fear tells you to stop.
When you look in the mirror and judge yourself harshly.
When life changes and you feel unprepared.
When you fail and the inner critic becomes loud.
When you are grieving a life you thought you would have.

Self love shows up in all those moments.

Every time life has pushed me to change, the practice of self love has helped me stand back up. It helped me pivot into a new career. It helped me heal from trauma. It helped me learn how to be gentle with myself as a mother. It helped me trust my own decisions. It helped me build a career I adore. It helped me rebuild my identity after losing the first one.

Self love is not only the foundation of healing. It is the foundation of becoming.

Becoming a therapist deepened my understanding even more. Therapy taught me that people are not broken. They are wounded. And wounds can heal when treated with consistency, compassion, and care. Therapy taught me that most people are harder on themselves than anyone else has ever been. Therapy taught me that the human mind is wired to survive, not thrive, unless you teach it how.

And self love is the tool that teaches your mind how.

Self love also teaches you boundaries. Many people believe boundaries are selfish, but they are actually acts of respect. They protect your inner world. They define what you can and cannot give. They help you build relationships that are healthy. Boundaries are not walls. They are doorways that allow the right things in and keep the harmful things out.

I used to give so much of myself that I had nothing left. I thought giving endlessly made me kind. I thought saying yes made me valuable. But self love taught me that boundaries are not barriers. They are bridges to better relationships.

You cannot love yourself if you do not protect your peace.

Self love also shows up in the way you talk to yourself. Self talk is one of the most powerful forces in your mind. The words you repeat become the beliefs you carry. Many people speak to themselves in ways they would never speak to anyone else. They criticize their bodies, doubt their worth, and call themselves failures. These patterns are learned, and they can be unlearned.

Self love transforms your self talk. It turns your inner voice into a supportive guide instead of a harsh critic. It teaches you to ask, "What would I say to someone I care about who felt this way?" and then say the same to yourself.

Another important part of daily self love is learning to rest. Rest is not laziness. Rest is repair. When you deny yourself rest, you deny yourself healing. You cannot pour from an empty cup. You cannot be resilient if you are running on fumes. You cannot grow if you are too tired to stand.

Rest is part of the work.

Self love also requires compassion toward your past self. Many people look back on their choices with shame. They judge themselves for not knowing better. But the truth is simple. You did your best with the tools you had at the time. Self love honors that. It says, "I forgive myself for what I did not know. I release the shame I no longer need to carry."

One of the most life changing lessons I learned is this: You cannot punish yourself into becoming a better person. You can only love yourself into becoming one.

Self love invites you to grow without fear. It teaches you that you are capable of change. It teaches you that mistakes do not define you. It teaches you that your value is not tied to performance. It teaches you that it is safe to evolve. It teaches you that joy is possible.

Above all, self love teaches you that you are worthy of the life you are trying to build.

Radical Acceptance, Pivoting, and the Journey From Surviving to Thriving

One of the most powerful parts of self love is learning radical acceptance. People often misunderstand this idea. They think acceptance means approval or surrender or pretending everything is fine. But radical acceptance is very different. It is the decision to acknowledge reality instead of fighting it. It is the courage to face what you cannot change. It is the strength to release the belief that you could have done something differently.

Radical acceptance is a doorway. It is the moment you stop resisting and start healing.

I had to learn radical acceptance in one of the hardest chapters of my life. My body was done. My marriage was over. My career had ended long before I was ready for it to. My heart was broken. I was raising two children alone. I was grieving my dream, grieving the person I thought I would be, and grieving the life I imagined I would have.

I was truly a victim in many parts of my story.I believed I needed to fix everything that hurt. I believed if I tried hard enough, I could reverse reality. Then, I could have my old life back.

Radical acceptance taught me that I could not rewrite the past. I could only choose what it meant moving forward.

In order for me to thrive, I had to stop trying to let go of the pain and instead accept what it was. Letting go implies that you can erase what happened. Acceptance says that you honor what happened while refusing to let it define your future. Acceptance allowed me to rewrite the narrative of my life. It gave me the freedom to decide what these experiences would mean for me.

I knew I did not want to be a survivor forever. The word survivor felt heavy on my body. It felt like a label people gave me for making it through something awful. It felt like it kept me connected to the people or events that hurt me. I had survived, yes, but I did not want the story of survival to be the story of who I was.

I wanted to be a thriver.

But thriving requires grieving.

People often rush past grief because it is uncomfortable. They want solutions, not sorrow. They want quick fixes. They want happiness now. But if you refuse to grieve the life you lost, you cannot make space for the life you deserve.

I had to grieve the dream I had held for so long. I had to grieve the ballerina I believed I would become. I had to grieve the family I imagined I would build. I had to grieve the body that betrayed me. I had to grieve the choices I made and the ones I never had the chance to make. I had to grieve the future that vanished overnight.

Grief is not a sign of weakness. Grief is a sign that something mattered.

Allowing myself to grieve opened the door to a new life. When you do not grieve, you hold on. When you hold on, you make no room for what is meant for you next. If you hold on to the loss, you close the door to a prettier future. Acceptance does not mean forgiving the people who hurt you. It means no longer being tied to the power or control they once had.

Radical acceptance freed me.

It allowed me to say, This is what happened. This is what I lived through. This is what shaped me. And this is what I choose to do with it now. That choice became the foundation of my healing.

This is also the heart of post-traumatic growth.

People often assume trauma only destroys. But trauma can also transform. Post-traumatic growth happens when you allow yourself to learn from what you lived through. It does not minimize the pain. It simply refuses to let the pain be the final chapter. Growth comes when you ask, How do I become the person I am meant to be because of this, not despite this.

My role as a therapist is to walk with people through that very question.

Every person I work with has survived something. A heartbreak. A betrayal. A shattered dream. Illness. Anxiety. Depression. Loneliness. Guilt. Shame. Loss. Each story is different, but the human heart responds in similar ways. We shut down. We avoid. We harden. We blame ourselves. We collapse. We isolate. We doubt our worth.

And yet, every single one of these people is capable of thriving.

Thriving means accepting what is, releasing what was, and choosing what will be.

Thriving means you take the pieces of your past and build something beautiful with them.

Thriving means you no longer live in reaction to your pain.

Thriving means your trauma does not get the last word.

Thriving means you reclaim your voice.

Thriving means you learn to trust yourself again.

Thriving means your worth is not up for debate.

One of the things I tell my clients often is this: You do not have to be who you were yesterday. You are allowed to change. You are allowed to evolve. You are allowed to become someone new. You are allowed to want more for yourself. Your past experiences shaped you, but they do not have power over who you get to be tomorrow.

This is especially important for women, because in our society, the older we get, the more invisible we become. When we are young, we are valued for beauty. When we are older, we are judged for aging. We are told we are either too much or not enough. We are judged if we get Botox and judged if we do not. We are expected to raise children as if we have no career and build careers as if we have no children. The older we get, the more we are told our value declines.

But self love teaches you something very different.

Self love reminds you that your value does not increase when you are thin, young, productive, or quiet. Your value does not decrease when you age, rest, or change your mind. Self love teaches you that your worth is constant because it is internal, not external.

Aging does not make you less. Aging makes you more.

More aware. More grounded. More wise. More compassionate. More connected to what truly matters.

Self love shifts the narrative from "I am running out of time" to "I am becoming more myself."

Pivoting becomes easier when you stop tying your identity to one single path. My injury forced me into a pivot I never wanted. My divorce forced me into a pivot I never expected. My trauma forced me into a pivot I never prepared for. But every pivot led me to the next version of myself.

People think the bravest thing you can do is stay. But the bravest thing is often changing direction.

The art of the pivot is not about giving up. It is about recognizing when one chapter has ended and choosing to write the next one with intention.

Pivoting is a form of self love.

It is the moment you choose growth instead of stagnation.
It is the moment you choose to let go of what is hurting you.
It is the moment you choose to redefine success on your own terms.
It is the moment you choose to become the person your future needs.

When I decided to become a therapist, it was one of the biggest acts of self love in my life. I did not know if I would be good at it. I did not know if I would succeed. I had no guarantee that this new path would work out. But something in me knew that healing others would help heal the parts of myself I had ignored.

I discovered that therapy is not about me. It is about the person in front of me. In dance, I could hide behind characters. In therapy, I hide behind service. I get to be the safe place I once needed. I get to help others make sense of their lives. I get to support them as they break the patterns that kept them small. I get to witness the moment someone realizes they are worthy.

My love for therapy comes from the love I had to learn for myself.

I am not perfect. I still wake up some mornings forgetting I am no longer a dancer. I still have old patterns that try to resurface. I still experience fear, doubt, and frustration. But self love has given me the tools to move through those moments gently. I give myself grace. I breathe. I ground myself. I remember that self love is not a destination. It is a daily commitment.

I am the sum of all my experiences, good, bad, and indifferent. They shaped me, but they do not control me. Tomorrow I will wake up a little different, and that is the beauty of being human.

Self love has turned every part of my story into something meaningful.

And it can do the same for you.

Becoming the Person You Were Meant to Be

Self love is not the end of your journey. It is the beginning of the life you were always meant to live. So many people think self love is a final destination, a place you reach once you are healed, successful, peaceful, or confident. But the truth is that self love is the practice that gets you there. Self love is the path, not the finish line.

When I look back on my life, I can see the turning points clearly. I can see the moments where everything fell apart. I can see the moments when I felt lost, unseen, overwhelmed, or defeated. I can see the patterns I once lived inside without even realizing I was trapped. But I can also see the moments when I stood up. I can see the moments I said enough. I can see the moments I walked away from what was hurting me. I can see the moments where self love quietly stepped in before I had words for it.

Every major transformation in my life came from self love.

It came from the moment I allowed myself to grieve.
It came from the moment I allowed myself to rest.
It came from the moment I admitted I needed help.
It came from the moment I let myself break.
It came from the moment I started rebuilding with intention.
It came from the moment I forgave myself for not knowing what I know now.

Self love is the root of every healthy, stable, meaningful life. Without it, everything else collapses.

People often ask me how self love actually changes your life. They want proof that the hard work is worth it. And every client who has done this work knows the answer: self love changes how you see yourself. When you see yourself differently, you make different choices. You choose relationships that honor you. You choose boundaries that protect you. You choose careers that fulfill you. You choose environments that support you. You choose people who uplift you. You choose futures that excite you.

Self love is the foundation of good decision making.

When you believe you are unworthy, you accept situations that harm you.
When you believe you are replaceable, you let others treat you carelessly.
When you believe you are not enough, you exhaust yourself trying to prove your value.
When you believe you are broken, you sabotage your own healing.

But when you believe you are worthy, something shifts.

You become honest with yourself.
You stop chasing the approval of people who do not see your value.
You choose relationships that feel safe.
You stop apologizing for needing boundaries.
You stop abandoning yourself to keep others comfortable.
You stop shrinking.

You become exactly who you were always meant to be.

Self love also changes the way you face adversity. Trauma, heartbreak, disappointment, and failure no longer become signs that you are not enough. They become moments that reveal your strength. When you practice self love, you develop resilience. You learn that you can survive hard things. You learn that you can rebuild. You learn that you can trust yourself to make it through. You learn that pain is not a punishment but a teacher.

This is where thriving begins.

Thriving is not about having a perfect life. Thriving is about having the emotional tools to face imperfect moments. It is about grounding yourself. It is about catching your thoughts before they spiral. It is about choosing supportive beliefs. It is about knowing when to walk away. It is about saying, "This is not what I deserve." It is about saying, "There is nothing wrong with me." It is about saying, "I am allowed to want more."

Thriving happens when you accept your past without letting it control your future.

As I grew into my work as a therapist, I watched people transform right in front of me. People who walked into my office unsure of who they were began discovering their voice. People who once apologized for taking up space learned to stand firmly in who they are. People who once carried shame like a shadow learned to release it. People who once viewed themselves as broken learned to see themselves as whole.

Every one of these transformations began with self love.

This is why the Identify, Challenge, Replace framework is so essential. It teaches you to recognize the beliefs that limit you. It teaches you to challenge the thoughts that hurt you. It teaches you to replace those patterns with compassion. The more you practice this, the more your mind changes. The more your mind changes, the more your life changes. You do not have to force your healing. You guide it.

Self love is not loud. It is steady.

It is in the early morning breaths you take before the world wakes up.
It is in the first kind thought you offer yourself after a mistake.
It is in the moment you choose rest instead of punishment.
It is in the pause between an old pattern and a new choice.
It is in the gentle way you speak to yourself when you are hurting.
It is in the quiet decision to keep going even when it is hard.

Self love is the most powerful form of inner strength.

And then comes the most beautiful part: identity.

So many people believe their identity is fixed. They believe they must stay who they were at twenty, thirty, forty, or fifty. They believe they missed their chance at becoming the person they wanted to be. They believe they must stay loyal to the path they started even when that path no longer fits.

This is where self love becomes freedom.

Self love gives you permission to change.
Self love gives you permission to grow.
Self love gives you permission to reinvent.
Self love gives you permission to pivot at any age.

You are not limited by your past.

You are expanded by your future.

I had to learn this myself. I built an entire identity around being a dancer. I carried that identity like a second skin. Losing dance felt like losing myself. But self love taught me that identity is not what you do. Identity is who you choose to be.

I chose to be someone who helps others heal.

I chose to be someone who listens deeply.

I chose to be someone who teaches compassion.

I chose to be someone who guides people through their darkest seasons.

I chose to be someone who practices what she teaches.

Becoming a therapist was not a backup plan. It was the life I was meant to discover.

Every experience I lived — the injury, the grief, the trauma, the late nights studying, the heartbreak — prepared me for this work. Everything I thought had broken me actually rebuilt me. Everything I thought had ended my story actually redirected it.

This is the truth I want every reader to understand:

You are the sum of all your experiences, good, bad, and indifferent. They shaped you, but they do not own you. You are allowed to change your story. You are allowed to outgrow the life you thought you wanted. You are allowed to choose a different ending. You are allowed to become the person your past self needed.

Self love is not a luxury. It is the foundation of becoming.

It is the reason you will grow.
It is the reason you will heal.
It is the reason you will thrive.
It is the reason you will build a life that feels like home.

You are exactly where you need to be at this moment.
You are perfectly imperfect.
You are worthy of compassion.
You are capable of growth.
You are allowed to evolve.
You are allowed to take up space.
You are allowed to heal.
You are allowed to start again.
You are allowed to want a life that feels good.

And with self love, you will create it.

Chapter Five

The Labyrinth of Toxic Love: Recognizing and Reclaiming Yourself

By Nina Batista, MSW

A licensed clinical social worker who helps individuals navigate relationship struggles, trauma, and life transitions.

In the messy and unpredictable journey of life, there's this one ride we're all desperately signing up for—the pursuit of love. It's this hunger deep within, pushing us to seek something real, something that makes us feel seen, heard, and cherished. But let's be real, what the heck is real love? We're all suckers for sweet words, grand gestures, and that feeling of being on cloud nine. Who doesn't want to feel wanted and admired? However, how do we know if it's love or just someone trying to satisfy their ego?

Love, in its truest form, is a profound connection that goes beyond mere words or gestures. It's the feeling of being understood, respected, supported, and valued for who you are. It's not just about the grand romantic gestures or sweet nothings; real love is grounded in shared values, mutual respect, and a deep emotional bond. However, the confusion often creeps in when we mistake the surface-level intensity of infatuation for the depth of genuine love. The longing for acceptance and companionship can blind us to red flags, making it easy to get lost in the whirlwind of attention and affection.

It's like trying to navigate a maze where the boundaries between authentic love and deceptive allure become blurred, leaving us susceptible to the pitfalls of misguided emotions.

Stepping into the complex realm of dating goes beyond mere surface-level attractions; it's a nuanced exploration of the person behind the smiles. We scrutinize not only physical appeal but also character, kindness, and overall demeanor. The challenge arises as dating isn't a simple stroll but rather a tightrope walk over the chasm of uncertainty. Deciphering if the person across from us is genuinely good at heart, not just charming on the surface, becomes the quest. However, this journey becomes even more intricate when the dating landscape transforms into a minefield, concealing red flags adeptly.

In the pursuit of love, we may encounter skillful pretenders and adept liars who cleverly hide warning signs. Navigating this tricky balancing act requires remaining open-hearted yet vigilant, hoping to decipher the complexities of dating without falling prey to the artful deception that can lurk beneath the surface.

This exploration of the dating landscape hits home, as my own pursuit of love led me down an unforeseen path, earning me a self-initiated Ph.D. in Narcissism. The enchanting allure of the love bombing stage marked the beginning—an artfully crafted phase where illusions seemed to manifest effortlessly. Vivid memories linger from our initial encounter, where he painted a world with me as the sole inhabitant, the most captivating woman he had ever encountered. His promise of shared values forged an unspoken bond, and each moment felt like a cherished blessing. Amidst this intoxicating brew of feeling wanted, secure, loved, sexy, and irresistibly desirable, I found myself captivated by a surreal high, unable to resist.

Little did I know, this enchantment was merely the prelude to a tumultuous journey, as the ecstasy of love morphed into the shadows of manipulation.

So, fast forward a few months, and I started sensing this weird shift. The guy who once made me feel like I was the queen of the world suddenly had me questioning everything I did or said. It began subtly, with remarks like, "Hmm, you're wearing that?" while I was getting ready for our date night. But then, it escalated to a point where he'd yell, "Get off me!" while literally pushing me away during a moment I was trying to initiate some intimacy—no explanation. Yeah, you read that right—I'm trying to be all sexy, kissing his neck, and he treats me like I'm some annoying pest. I'd end up in tears, questioning why he didn't want to be close anymore, and guess what his brilliant response was? He blamed me.

According to him, I wasn't putting in any effort. "You didn't even get a manicure. You don't make me want to do nice things for you," he'd yell. And get this: apparently, he suddenly didn't have that high of a sex drive. Now, let me tell you, this wasn't just a normal dry spell or the occasional "not in the mood" day—this was happening way too often. When I'd try to speak to him about it, silence. I'd ask him if everything was okay or how I could support him, and his response? "You're not my therapist."

Now, as a self-reflective, compassionate person, this had me going through our entire relationship questioning if I was crossing any boundaries between my career and my relationship! I'd burst into tears, stop engaging in conversation with him, and he'd come over, hug me, all the while laughing, telling me he loves his "babers" and doesn't want to see me cry. It felt like he enjoyed seeing me emotionally distraught from his rejection. Naturally, I started to isolate a bit, not initiating physical intimacy as often, and like clockwork, he'd start kissing me and wanting to get intimate.

So, what did this teach me? If I just stay quiet, don't initiate, I get rewarded. If I express my needs, I get punished.

Basically, the emotional rollercoaster I endured became his messed-up version of foreplay. The next day, he'd buy me flowers, act all sweet, and give me glimpses of the guy I fell in love with—a toxic cycle that left me feeling like I was losing my mind. He conditioned me to be grateful for mediocre treatment. The bare minimum.

To make things more confusing for me, he was a different person in front of our friends. Like this sweet angel sent from heaven—affectionate, loving, caring. Some of our pals would even tell me how lucky I was to be with him, gushing about how much he adored me. Fast forward to when it was just the two of us in the car, and bam! It's like Mr. Jekyll and Hyde decided to make an appearance. He'd turn ice cold, yelling at me for singing in the car because apparently, I was "ruining the song." It left me feeling beyond confused, but now I get it. It was all about protecting his image, putting on this front for an audience.

Then comes the real kicker. "You don't make me want to make an effort. You didn't even get your nails done. You gained weight. Why would I want to have sex with you? It's like you completely gave up on our relationship," he'd shout as I tried to talk about my feelings. And if that wasn't enough, the stonewalling would kick in—the cold, hard ignoring treatment. Cue my anxiety shooting through the roof as I questioned every word I just said. Was I making a big deal out of nothing? "Maybe he's right," I'd think to myself.

I became conditioned to stop expressing when something bothered me because if I did, he'd blame me, pick a fight, or give me the silent treatment for hours.

The real kicker was the torture of having the love of your life intentionally withhold affection as a form of punishment—just because I wasn't behaving the way he wanted. Everything had to be on his terms. And any time I dared to point that out, he'd hit me with the "selfish" label, throwing around every negative word that he was actually embodying. It was like living in a twisted reality where up was down, and wrong was right.

He never respected my boundaries and would blame me for everything.

Keeping Your Voice and Words

I was incredibly confused. I blamed myself, falling into the trap of his narrative that I was too much, too negative, and ungrateful. It felt like every cutting remark and belittling comment carved deep into my self-esteem. The weight of his judgments became the lens through which I saw myself, distorting my perception until I couldn't even recognize the confident, capable person I used to be.

His accusations echoed relentlessly in my mind, a constant barrage of reasons why I wasn't enough. The harder I tried to meet his ever-changing expectations, the further I drifted from my authentic self. It was like a twisted dance where I was constantly questioning if I was too much or not enough, swinging between extremes dictated by his manipulative narrative.

The Cloak of Negativity

The negativity and "ungrateful" label wrapped around me like a heavy cloak I couldn't shake. Every time I tried to express my feelings or stand up for myself, it was met with dismissal and blame. I got stuck in a cycle of self-blame, convinced I held the key to unlocking the love and approval he had once showered on me. Little did I realize that by internalizing his narrative, I was letting him mold me into a version of myself that served his purpose—a puppet dancing to the strings of his emotional manipulation.

I bent over backward, trying to get him to give me any sliver of affection. I couldn't understand why our relationship was crumbling when the answer was right in front of me. We don't talk enough about personality disorders or emotional abuse in graduate school. In society, we hear "domestic violence," and we think of physical bruises. But what about when the violence is psychological?

In this distorted reality, my worth was tied entirely to his approval. Chasing his validation became suffocating, leaving me breathless under the constant weight of trying to fit into the mold he decided was acceptable. His manipulation became a silent poison, eating away at the foundation of my self-worth, until I couldn't tell where his story ended and my identity began.

Why I Stayed

You might wonder why I stayed. Leaving a narcissist isn't like a regular breakup—it's like trying to break free from an addiction. It's profoundly challenging and traumatic, stretching over months or even years. You're trauma bonded to them, addicted to their approval. Financial abuse, where they control every household decision, and a lack of alternative support systems make leaving even harder.

It's also nearly impossible to grasp that the person who was once the love of your life is now intentionally abusing you. Your soulmate has become your abuser—how do you even begin to wrap your brain around that? As a self-reflective, compassionate person and a therapist, I wanted to see the good in him. Maybe he acted this way because of his own childhood trauma (and there was a lot of it). I made excuses for his behavior, convincing myself that if I just loved him enough, I could save him. But our relationship wasn't crumbling—he was deliberately destroying it.

The Fear of Leaving

The desire to leave burned inside me. I hated him, yet I couldn't bring myself to sever ties. The idea of life without him felt impossible, fed by his constant reminders that no one else would ever put up with me.

Leaving a narcissistic relationship is no small feat—it's not just about courage. Before this, I couldn't imagine enduring such treatment. I believed I was strong enough to leave if someone ever treated me poorly. But when you're trapped in a narcissistic relationship, the rules change entirely. The act of leaving becomes an almost insurmountable challenge, testing every ounce of your self-worth.

I tried to leave many times. I remember one moment clearly, about two months before we finally broke up. I was at home meditating, and it hit me—I didn't like the person I had become. I had lost myself. The future I'd once envisioned wasn't even mine anymore; it was dictated entirely by him. I realized I was nothing but a shell of the person I used to be.

I told him I was unhappy and wanted to leave, but when you reveal your intentions to a narcissist, they fight back hard. It triggers their hoovering—a desperate attempt to regain control. Trying to leave before they're ready sends them into overdrive because control is everything to them.

Narcissists use people to validate their insecurities. Their self-loathing is so deep that they project it onto others, turning them into mere objects to manipulate. It's like they're vampires, draining their victims of life while moving on to their next unsuspecting target.

The Illusion of Change

When I said it was over, he morphed back into the man I had fallen in love with—the one who would do anything to save the relationship. He suggested couples therapy, talked about me being the mother of his child, and showed glimpses of the guy I adored. It gave me hope, but it was all a facade to keep me around while he crafted his exit plan.

That hope became a trap. I clung to his promises, unaware that he was already lining up his next supply. When he finally left, it was for someone new. On my dead brother's birthday, no less. And to twist the knife, he ended things with a text—a single sentence after four years of psychological torment: "This isn't working out anymore. We're done."

But here's the kicker—my story isn't unique. It's one that countless women could tell. Swap the names, and you'd hear this same tale echoing across generations.

In the end, his leaving was the silver lining I couldn't see at first. It hurt—God, did it hurt—but once I came out of the fog, I saw the freedom waiting on the other side.

We don't recognize these relationships while we're in them. We normalize the toxicity, make excuses, and protect our partner's image, wanting to believe in their potential. But the truth is, nearly 1 in 4 women will navigate the treacherous waters of emotional abuse in their lifetimes.

Sharing My Story

I turned to social media to cope. I posted a video about my experience with my abuser, and overnight, it went viral—800,000 views and hundreds of thousands of comments saying things like, "I feel like you just summed up my entire relationship." That's when I realized—this is an epidemic. Wolves are preying on victims every day, disguised as sheep.

To make sense of it all, I dove into research. I devoured books on pathological lovers and emotional abuse. I trained with the Association of Psychopathic Survivors and found strength in connecting with others who had lived through similar experiences.

Understanding the Stages

The emotional scars I carried pushed me to explore what I'd been through. I realized my story wasn't unique—it was just one chapter in a larger narrative of emotional abuse. To process my pain and help others, I began breaking down the stages of dating a narcissist. Little did I know how cathartic it would be or how many lives it might impact.

For me, there were seven distinct stages:

The Love Bombing Stage

The Devaluation Stage

The Self-Blame Stage

The Not Being Able to Leave Stage

The Hoover Stage

The Discard Stage

The Healing Stage

Stage 1: The Love Bombing Stage

Dating a narcissist starts with an extravagant performance. They make you feel like the center of their world, showering you with compliments, affection, and attention. It's intoxicating, like a whirlwind romance designed to pull you in.

But beneath the surface lies manipulation. Their goal isn't connection—it's control. They mirror your desires, pretending to share your values and interests to gain your trust. It's not love; it's a calculated game to make you dependent on their approval.

This phase is like a dopamine rush, creating an emotional high that blinds you to red flags. As their true nature starts to emerge—gaslighting, criticism, and isolation—your brain craves the euphoria of those early days, trapping you in their cycle of manipulation.

They condition you to comply with their expectations, rewarding "good" behavior and punishing anything that challenges their control. Over time, you stop expressing your needs, afraid of triggering their wrath. The love bombing stage sets the stage for a toxic and controlling relationship.

The Self-Blame Stage

This stage feels like a disorienting labyrinth, where confusion and self-blame take over. The relationship that once seemed so clear becomes murky, leaving you lost and grappling with a distorted sense of self. You find yourself consumed by an overwhelming need to please your narcissistic partner, even at your own expense.

The narcissist flips the narrative, making you believe you're the problem—too much, too negative, too ungrateful. Their cutting remarks and belittling comments carve deep into your self-esteem, distorting your perception of yourself until you barely recognize the confident, capable person you used to be.

Their accusations echo in your mind, creating a relentless loop of self-doubt and criticism. The harder you try to meet their impossible expectations, the further you stray from your authentic self. It becomes a twisted dance where you constantly question whether you're too much or not enough, trapped in the manipulative story they've written for you.

Labels like "too much" or "ungrateful" weigh heavily, impossible to shake. Every time you express your feelings or stand up for yourself, you're met with dismissal or blame, reinforcing a cycle of self-blame. You start to believe that if you can just fix yourself, you'll unlock the love they once gave so freely. But in surrendering to their narrative, you lose pieces of your identity, becoming a puppet to their manipulation.

Your self-worth becomes tied to their approval. You exhaust yourself trying to fit into the mold they've created, only to feel breathless under the weight of constantly striving for their validation. The insidious nature of their manipulation makes it hard to see where their narrative ends and your real self begins.

The Not Being Able to Leave Stage

This stage is marked by an overwhelming sense of entrapment and loneliness. Even when you know something is fundamentally wrong, you're caught in a web of manipulation that feels impossible to escape.

It's a paradox. Your instincts scream that the relationship is toxic, yet a mix of dependency and isolation leaves you feeling stuck. The narcissist's emotional manipulation erodes your self-worth, making you believe you need them for validation.

Loneliness becomes a constant companion as the narcissist isolates you from friends and family. Those who once offered support are pushed away, leaving you without a safety net. The more isolated you feel, the more reliant you become on the narcissist.

Even with the awareness that the relationship is damaging, the ability to leave is stifled by a sense of helplessness. You feel adrift, lost in a distorted version of reality where the rules keep shifting. The emotional weight of being trapped adds another layer of confusion and pain.

This stage is a profound internal struggle, where the emotional bonds created with the narcissist make it hard to see the relationship for what it truly is. The more you try to reconcile your intuition with your feelings of entrapment, the harder it becomes to break free.

The Hoover Stage

The hoover stage begins when you try to leave the relationship. It's like watching a carefully crafted play, with the narcissist bringing back the persona that initially drew you in.

When you declare the relationship is over, the narcissist pulls out all the stops. They become the charming, attentive partner you fell in love with, promising change and a brighter future together. They might suggest therapy, paint a picture of a life you once dreamed of, and promise to be everything you wanted.

But this stage is a tactical maneuver. It's not about genuine change or reconciliation—it's about control. The narcissist uses this facade to reel you back in, buying themselves more time to maintain their dominance in the relationship.

For the person on the receiving end, this stage is emotionally exhausting. Seeing glimpses of the person you once loved reignites hope, creating an inner struggle that's hard to navigate. But the hoover stage is nothing more than a calculated act to regain control. Recognizing this manipulation and prioritizing your well-being becomes essential for breaking free from their grip.

The Discard Stage

Experiencing the discard stage in a relationship with a narcissist feels like having the rug pulled out from under you. It's abrupt, heart-wrenching, and leaves you questioning the very ground you stood on. One moment, you're wrapped in their charm and affection; the next, you're tossed aside like an afterthought. The person who once felt like the center of your world becomes elusive, disappearing without explanation, leaving you grappling with a gaping void.

What makes this stage so devastating is the lightning-fast shift from intense closeness to icy detachment. It's bewildering—one day, you're the center of their universe; the next, you're met with silence. Calls go unanswered, messages ignored. After they've extracted all the emotional satisfaction they need or found their next target, they vanish without warning, leaving you drowning in confusion and heartbreak.

The aftermath of the discard stage feels like navigating emotional ruins. You're left facing betrayal, rejection, and the haunting question of "why?" While you're piecing together your shattered self-esteem, the narcissist, devoid of empathy, swiftly moves on to their next conquest. The realization that their abandonment wasn't about any personal flaw, but rather a reflection of their internal emptiness, becomes a crucial step toward healing. It's painful, but it marks the beginning of reclaiming your identity from the wreckage of a relationship built on illusions.

The Healing Stage

Navigating the healing stage after being entangled with a narcissist feels like moving through a dense emotional fog. The scars left by the discard stage run deep, and healing becomes a process of slowly piecing together a shattered mosaic of yourself. It begins with acknowledging the pain, accepting the reality of the relationship, and gradually releasing the emotional baggage that weighs you down.

Healing is not a linear journey; it's marked by both victories and setbacks. Rediscovering your inner strength is pivotal. Embracing the vulnerabilities that were exploited, you begin to understand that these do not define you. Building a support network of trusted friends, family, or professionals becomes essential. Their understanding and encouragement act as a balm for the wounds inflicted during the chaotic dance with a narcissist.

As you continue through the healing stage, self-compassion becomes your ally. It's about treating yourself with kindness, recognizing that healing takes time, and allowing yourself space to process the emotions that surface. Reconnecting with passions, rediscovering interests that were overshadowed, and setting firm boundaries are essential in cultivating a renewed sense of self. This process is about reclaiming your identity from the remnants of a relationship designed to diminish it.

What a Healthy Relationship Actually Looks Like

In reflecting on relationships, the stark contrast between healthy and toxic bonds becomes apparent. A healthy relationship is a sanctuary, built on mutual respect, trust, communication, support, and emotional well-being. In contrast, a toxic relationship fosters harmful dynamics that inflict emotional damage. Here are the hallmarks of a healthy relationship:

Communication: Healthy relationships thrive on open, honest, and respectful communication. Both partners feel safe expressing their thoughts and emotions, and conflicts are resolved constructively. Disagreements feel like a team effort to tackle the issue, not a battle against each other.

Respect and Boundaries: Mutual respect is foundational in a healthy relationship. Each partner honors boundaries, values, and individuality, supporting one another's growth and independence.

Trust: Trust is the cornerstone of a healthy bond. It fosters security and reliability, with both partners demonstrating trustworthiness.

Support and Empathy: In healthy relationships, partners offer encouragement and empathy, being there for each other through challenges with emotional and practical support.

Equality and Power Dynamics: Decisions are made collaboratively, and power is shared equally. Both partners feel valued as individuals with equal say in the relationship.

Emotional Well-being: A healthy relationship promotes happiness and personal growth. It's a space for vulnerability, self-expression, and emotional intimacy, where both individuals flourish.

Understanding these distinctions provides a roadmap for cultivating a thriving connection. It's a journey toward a partnership built on love and respect, allowing both individuals to grow authentically.

While relationships are complex, focusing on overall patterns and dynamics is key. If you find yourself in a toxic relationship, prioritize your well-being. Reach out to trusted friends, family, or professionals. Remember, you don't have to navigate the path to a healthier connection alone.

The Common Red Flags

Toxic relationships manifest in patterns that drain emotional energy and harm your well-being. These dynamics often involve justifying your partner's behavior or shielding their actions from loved ones. Here are some common red flags:

Lack of Respect: Disregard for boundaries, dismissing opinions, or belittling feelings. Discussions often lead to arguments, causing you to stop sharing your thoughts.

Control and Manipulation: Monitoring your activities, isolating you from support, or making unilateral decisions. Manipulation through guilt or threats creates a constant sense of walking on eggshells.

Constant Criticism: Undermining your worth by focusing on flaws and mistakes. Criticism becomes a tool for control, eroding self-esteem.

Lack of Trust: Constant suspicion, baseless accusations, and invasive behaviors like checking your phone.

Emotional or Physical Abuse: Gaslighting, demeaning behavior, or physical harm. Emotional abuse can be just as damaging as physical abuse.

Constant Negativity: A pervasive negative atmosphere that leaves you drained and on edge. Cognitive dissonance makes you feel trapped—unable to leave, yet suffocated by staying.

Circular Conversations: Conversations that go nowhere, filled with tangents and irrelevant remarks, leaving you emotionally exhausted.

Recognizing these red flags is crucial in breaking free from a toxic dynamic.

Boundaries: The Cornerstone of Healthy Relationships

Boundaries are the silent architects of healthy and respectful connections. They act as vital guidelines, defining acceptable behaviors, personal limits, and preferences.

Setting boundaries ensures individuality, autonomy, and emotional well-being. They are the protective guardrails of relationships, maintaining balance and mutual respect.

Emotional Boundaries: Respecting feelings, opinions, and values. Openly communicating emotional needs fosters mutual understanding.

Physical Boundaries: Setting limits on physical touch and intimacy. Respecting personal space and comfort levels is essential.

Time and Independence Boundaries: Balancing personal time and shared moments ensures individual growth alongside the relationship.

Communication Boundaries: Establishing respectful communication practices like active listening and avoiding harmful language.

Maintaining boundaries requires open dialogue and mutual respect, but they are essential for creating a safe and supportive relationship.

Establishing Boundaries

Establishing boundaries is essential for maintaining individuality, autonomy, and emotional well-being. They act as protective guardrails in a relationship, ensuring a safe and secure journey for both partners. Here are some examples of boundaries in a romantic relationship:

Emotional Boundaries:

Each partner has the right to their feelings, opinions, and values. Respecting and validating each other's emotions without dismissing or belittling them is critical. Emotional boundaries involve recognizing and communicating personal needs and fostering a willingness to understand each other's perspectives. For instance, if you want to discuss a tough day at work and your partner seems uninterested, addressing that disinterest respectfully upholds emotional boundaries.

Physical Boundaries:

Physical boundaries involve setting limits on touch and intimacy, allowing each partner to decide their comfort levels. These boundaries may include preferences about public displays of affection, personal space, or sexual activities. For example, expressing intolerance for physical violence or stating discomfort with certain sexual activities helps define physical boundaries.

Time and Independence Boundaries:

Respecting personal space and individual pursuits is vital for balancing the relationship and maintaining separate identities. For instance, choosing to spend an evening with friends instead of your partner exemplifies a healthy independence boundary.

Communication Boundaries:

Communication boundaries establish respectful practices like active listening and honest, kind conversations while avoiding harmful behaviors like shouting or name-calling. For example, explicitly stating that name-calling is unacceptable strengthens communication boundaries.

Maintaining boundaries requires open and honest communication, active listening, and mutual understanding. Regular check-ins ensure boundaries are respected and allow for adjustments as needed.

The Cycle of Toxic Relationships

In toxic relationships, the cycle of inconsistency becomes addictive. It's the allure of a perpetual "maybe" that keeps us hooked, much like a gambler chasing a win at a slot machine. The highs of love-bombing flood your brain with dopamine, creating an intoxicating high that makes walking away feel impossible.

Picture a casino: each win, no matter how small, feels exhilarating, even if it's just $5. As losses mount, the compulsion to keep playing grows. Similarly, in a toxic relationship, even the smallest gesture of affection after a withdrawal feels rewarding. This fleeting satisfaction keeps you yearning, despite the mounting emotional cost.

The difficulty in leaving stems from a lingering desire for that affection, confusion over its sudden absence, and the internalized belief that you're to blame for the change. Cognitive dissonance emerges, grappling with opposing beliefs: knowing the relationship is harmful yet feeling incapable of imagining life without it. Gaslighting further distorts reality, fostering doubt and confusion.

Recognizing the futility of changing a toxic person is a critical realization. Control lies in our responses and what we are willing or unwilling to tolerate. This is where boundaries become vital. Without clear boundaries, confusion thrives, and resentment festers. Communicating these limits is crucial; breaches leave us feeling dismissed. Boundaries become the decision point: to continue with someone who disregards them or to prioritize our well-being.

Recognizing and enforcing boundaries is not just self-preservation—it's a declaration of self-worth. It allows us to navigate toxic relationships with clarity, paving the way for healing and growth.

From Euphoria to Anguish: Breaking Free from Toxic Love

Recognizing the toxic threads woven into a relationship can feel like navigating a labyrinth, especially when emotions run deep, and love clouds judgment. Acknowledging the warning signs is daunting, often avoided out of fear—fear of losing the relationship, fear of being alone, or fear that another soulmate may never come along.

Toxicity rarely announces itself; instead, it sneaks into the romantic stages, cloaked in a love story. During the love-bombing stage, it feels euphoric, convincing you that you've found your soulmate within weeks. You dream of a shared future, and the thought of life without them becomes unthinkable.

Then the insidious shift begins. Subtle jabs imply wrongdoing without clarity. Walking on eggshells becomes routine—a cautious dance to keep the peace. The confusion deepens when the person who celebrated your perfection begins criticizing the very traits they once adored. Expressing feelings is met with blame-shifting, making you the unwitting cause of every conflict.

Breaking free from toxicity requires courage and self-reflection. It's about reclaiming the pieces of yourself, rediscovering strength, and practicing self-compassion. Recognizing the shifts from euphoria to anguish is the first step toward liberation, paving the way for a future free from the chains of a toxic past.

Chapter Six

A Recipe for a Fulfilling Intimate Life: Getting Comfortable with Uncomfortable Intimacy

By Dr. Randi Reichel Fournier, DMFT, LMFT, M.Ed.

A therapist and relationship coach who helps individuals and couples navigate sexual health, deepen emotional intimacy, and build more confident, fulfilling connections.

My partner and I are both aware that a sex life can be satisfying and that sometimes satisfaction may lead to routine sex. Things that work and feel good lead to more of the same, which can eventually feel monotonous. With a goal of being proactive, we decided to get more intentional about switching things up a bit.

Breaking the Routine: Exploring Intentional Intimacy

As we put our spontaneity (and a burrito-print sleep mask) to good use, he focused on me without allowing me to return any favors. My senses were heightened as they compensated for my inability to see. The darkness behind the mask was comfortable, and I liked the suspense of what I would feel next. After about five minutes of bliss, there was silence, a shift in his weight, and BOOM!

It was unexpected and unintentional, but as he shifted his positioning and swung his leg with force, he kneed me directly in the face. We both paused for a second in shock. As he apologized profusely, I took off the mask and ensured there were no lacerations or nosebleeds. I had to accept that my face would throb for a bit and that the probability of a black eye in my future was likely.

Of course, a knee to the face will usually change the mood of a sexual experience—it was not sexy. In that moment, we had a choice between feeling embarrassed and awkward, letting the time go to waste, or recognizing that unexpected things happen during sex. We laughed hysterically for a few minutes. After we got the giggles out, we brainstormed what I would tell people when they asked about my bruise and then continued our experience with a funny story to tell.

Did it take some time to shift gears and get back to where we were in terms of arousal? Yes. Was the experience exactly how it was before the knee to the face? Absolutely not. But that was okay! We maneuvered, pivoted, reset, and continued a very intimate moment that heightened our closeness and novelty.

Early Curiosity and Sexual Exploration

For as long as I can remember, the topic of sex was comfortable for me and one I loved discussing. The discovery of pornography (The Spice Channel), specifically in elementary school, propelled me into age-appropriate exploration that I attempted to make sense of in my own way.

The summer before middle school, my family friend Matt and I were watching *There's Something About Mary*. Of course,

I laughed enthusiastically during the scene where Ben Stiller's semen flies into Cameron Diaz's hair, and she mistakes it for hair gel. "Do you even know what that is?" Matt asked quizzically. "Yes, duh!" I replied, offended. I had absolutely no clue.

I've never been a good liar, so Matt gave me a quick anatomy lesson and explained what male masturbation was. I felt awkward, uncomfortable, and confused about this conversation—especially since Matt, who had admittedly touched his penis on a regular basis, had touched the dinner rolls 30 minutes prior. "Everyone does it," he said, "even your dad and brother." This statement put me over the edge and turned my discomfort into absolute dread. This could not be true. I'd never look at either of them the same again.

Developing a Sexual Narrative

Did the boys in my class touch their penises too? Did my gym teacher? Did my idol, John Travolta? What did all this mean? After taking some time to digest this information, my brain made connections between the Spice Channel and Matt's anatomy lesson. I needed to know and learn more, and so my research began.

Even as a child, I have been anything but shy and thrive on understanding people and things by asking detailed questions. I asked all my friends at school about masturbation and heard countless stories from different perspectives. Boys admitted to touching their penises shyly, triumphantly, proudly, and with stories of embarrassing and awkward moments to tell.

The Truth About Realistic Sex

Our country's health education system could benefit from a restructuring. What students learn is selective and often geared toward abstinence and the risks of sex rather than promoting healthy sex from an inclusive biopsychosocial approach. Missing from health class are conversations about the extremely important parts of sex: consent, boundaries, comfort, desires, arousal, and pleasure.

Parents often lack knowledge of how to properly discuss sex with their children. Without the full picture, many of us grew up learning about sex through forums available to us, the media, magazines, and pornography. This puts us at a disadvantage because the sex we see in movies and pornography is not indicative of realistic sex.

Let me set the stage: Two individuals burst into a home and cannot keep their hands off each other. They kiss passionately as they enter, while clothes come off, bodies are propped against the wall or kitchen counter, all while breathing audibly (but attractively). Eventually, they fall into bed for the best sex of their lives. Sound familiar?

The media's portrayal of sex undoubtedly sells sexy, and there's nothing wrong with that. However, it's important to recognize that media and pornographic sex is not realistic sex.

When we're unable to see media and pornography as fantasy, our perception of our sexual selves can cause challenges.

Sex is NOT always sexy! Realistic sex often entails figuring out comfortable positions, unexpected road bumps like falling off the bed, body parts not working as planned, and dealing with unique sounds, sweat, liquids, and goop. It's about interruptions, performance anxiety, and finding ways to connect even when things don't go as planned.

If we view realistic sex as a perfect way to gather information about ourselves and our partners, we open space for more sexual satisfaction, emotional intimacy, and relationship satisfaction.

A Spicy Anecdote

Here's a real-life example that provided many laughs between my friends and me (shared with permission):

When my friend and her husband were in the early stages of dating, they were fooling around, and foreplay began. After a minute of being fingered, she felt a burning sensation around her vulva that she had never experienced before, and they had to stop because it was getting intense.

Embarrassed, she expressed how he handed her an ice pack from his freezer. As they sat bewildered, they inspected her body, but nothing looked different. Suddenly, his eyes widened, his jaw dropped, and he said, "Ohhhhh noooo." He had made stuffed banana peppers for his family earlier that day and hadn't realized the heat from the peppers had lingered on his hands.

Talk about spicing things up.

Real-Life Interruptions

A friend of mine was getting sexy in the shower with her partner. As they navigated the water and limited space, she propped her hand on the soap dispenser, thinking more about pleasure and less about its ability to support her full body weight. Things happened quickly—her foot slipped, there was a huge crack, and down came the dispenser. Bodies desperately contorted to avoid falling. Luckily, she maintained her balance, staying upright, and the soap dispenser was the only casualty. The moment was interrupted, but they finished rinsing off and took their sexual experience to the bedroom instead.

Another friend explored a variety of positions with a long-term partner and queefed loudly, causing both to freeze in surprise. Mortified, she laughed nervously, hid her face in her hands, and stopped the moment. Vulnerable, she apologized for the interruption. Her partner, unfazed, acted like nothing happened and continued where they'd left off. This helped her feel comfortable in a moment of unexpected noises and recognize there was nothing to apologize for.

The Importance of Sexual Communication

My love for talking about sex didn't stop with my closest friends. Anyone I met with the potential for sexual relations heard a plethora of questions about my likes and dislikes. Partly, it's because I'm a planner—knowing what to expect on both ends made me feel comfortable. But talking about sex with the anticipation that it might happen also became a form of foreplay for me. As I gained more experience, the positive reinforcement of heightened sexual satisfaction encouraged me to continue these conversations.

Sexual communication, however, isn't always sexy. Discussing desires can feel intimidating because of the vulnerability it requires. Laying out our innermost wants leaves us open to judgment, embarrassment, or feelings of being "abnormal." For those raised in cultures or religions where sexual desires were shamed, this can lead to lingering confusion, ambivalence, or guilt about normal urges.

We're often conditioned to associate talking about sex with doing something wrong. Additionally, voicing what fulfills us sexually can spark anxiety about hurting our partner's pride. But this is where getting comfortable with discomfort comes in.

Starting a conversation by focusing on what you love about your sex life and expressing a genuine curiosity to learn more can help ease vulnerability. Open-ended questions like, "What was one of your favorite sexual experiences we've shared?" foster non-judgmental dialogue and build trust. Following up with questions like, "What made it memorable? What were your favorite parts? Is there something we could try more of from that experience?" encourages deeper understanding.

Recognizing and articulating desires, boundaries, likes, and dislikes strengthens emotional intimacy and improves sexual experiences. Get comfortable asking for what you want and sharing what you'd like to change.

Knowing Yourself First

Before you can communicate effectively about sex with a partner, you need to know what to talk about. Exploring your own needs, desires, and wants is key to a fulfilling sex life. While you can still enjoy sex without self-discovery, there's a great chance you might be missing out on aspects of intimacy that could enhance your experiences. Why not take your sex life to its fullest potential?

Learning what satisfies you most can be both fun and enlightening. You may discover surprising variables that play a role in your arousal, and you may also find that preferences change over time. Your wants and needs are unique, and that's completely normal.

For some, arousal can be spontaneous—nearly any context can spark desire. Picture your partner stepping out of the ocean, walking toward your towel, and you instantly want to have sex with them. If they were willing, you'd be ready immediately, perhaps even on the beach. Maybe you're watching your partner get ready for date night, and something about how they look in the mirror turns you on, prompting you to halt everything, dinner reservations be damned.

These spontaneous moments are often what we see in movies. However, most people experience something called responsive desire. Instead of arousal being immediate, it requires a slower buildup—playful conversation, cuddling, physical touch, or foreplay. Someone with responsive desire might see their partner step out of the ocean and think, "Wow, they look sexy," but arousal would follow later, perhaps after a meaningful conversation, a shared laugh, or kissing while applying sunblock.

Recognizing these differences can help normalize various experiences of desire, improve communication with your partner, and deepen your connection—both emotionally and physically.

Understanding the "Spark"

A common theme in discussions about sex and desire is the "spark." People often ask how to keep the spark alive or how to reignite it after marriage, babies, or the passage of time. It's important to reiterate that the "spark" we see in media isn't always realistic; in reality, the spark in a relationship is highly subjective. Just because you don't instantly want to have sex with your partner after seeing them step out of the ocean doesn't mean there isn't a spark.

Our culture places a lot of pressure on having a spark, yet fails to provide context about how human desire and arousal actually work. This can lead us to doubt ourselves, creating a slippery slope in understanding our feelings. I've personally experienced this in past relationships when I compared my attraction to unrealistic expectations.

If we believe that a spark (spontaneous desire) must always be present and don't feel it consistently—because many of us experience responsive desire instead—we may internalize the belief that something is wrong with us. This underscores the importance of understanding your sexual needs and desires. But where do you start?

Reflecting on Sexual Experiences

Imagine you're at the sex Olympics, about to crown your top three sexual endeavors. Stop and really think about who would place. Don't measure by the sex itself, but by the entire experience from start to finish. What do the winners have in common? Identifying common themes can help you understand the aspects of sex you gravitate toward and want more of.

Consider the following factors:

Relational factors: Elements tied to past relationships, such as trust, vulnerability, feelings of safety, and sexual skills.

Psychological and sociological factors: Influences from personal development and societal norms, such as education, sexual openness, personality, and body language.

Biological factors: How physical health, age, lifestyle, and even substance use impact sexual readiness and fulfillment.

Now, think about your worst sexual experiences and do the same. Analyze how those experiences influenced your readiness (or lack thereof) and which parts either excited or inhibited you. This process will help you understand what you enjoy, desire, and prefer during sex.

Communicating Desires

Once you've figured out your preferences, the next step is communicating them to your partner(s). This can feel daunting because sex is relational, and addressing issues requires mutual effort. Sexual obstacles are common, and intimacy and relationship stability may be threatened if they're ignored.

As humans, we fear rejection, and adding vulnerability to the mix can feel terrifying. However, you've already completed the first step by reflecting on your needs. Talking to friends about sex can be a helpful segue—it provides validation and laughs—but the deeper vulnerability comes in conversations with a partner.

Start by acknowledging any discomfort. For example, you might say, "This feels a little awkward for me, but I was hoping we could have an honest conversation about spicing up our sex life. Is there anything you'd be comfortable trying that we haven't done before?" Approaching the conversation with curiosity and openness helps your partner feel safe and prevents feelings of judgment.

Incorporating dialogue into sexual intimacy allows for assessment, practice, and feedback: "How was that for us? What should we consider next time?" These conversations should happen before, during, and after sex to build mutual understanding and closeness.

Navigating Boundaries and Vulnerability

Setting boundaries is crucial, especially with new partners. Conversations about comfort and expectations—such as openness to BDSM, role-playing, or limits—are best had beforehand. I learned this the hard way.

Once, while having sex for the first time with someone I met on a dating app, his hands moved to choke me. I don't enjoy being choked, so I immediately removed his hands and stated, "I don't like to be choked, so don't do that." He apologized and stopped, but choking is an intimate act that requires prior consent. That experience reinforced the importance of discussing boundaries before physical intimacy begins.

During sex, if you feel pain or discomfort, it's vital to express it immediately. However, many of us resist communicating in the moment for fear of ruining the mood or appearing less sexy. Put those thoughts aside and focus on how satisfying it can feel to own your desires and needs.

Embracing Imperfections

Sex is not always perfect, and orgasms are not the ultimate measure of good sex. The emphasis placed on orgasms can create performance anxiety, keeping us in our heads and away from the moment. Instead, focus on what feels good and on shared experiences, using communication to grow together.

For instance, an ex of mine lacked sexual experience, which was fine, but he never took the initiative to learn or ask questions about my preferences. The sex was repetitive and short-lived. After one particularly frustrating encounter, I initiated a conversation: "I was hoping we could discuss a few things about sex." I asked about his preferences, expressed my needs for foreplay and variety, and offered constructive feedback. While our sexual disconnect stemmed from deeper emotional intimacy issues, the conversation highlighted how important communication is for both physical and emotional connection.

Building a Strong Foundation

The beauty of sexual communication is its role as a tool for learning and growth. After trying something new, recapping the experience allows for honest feedback and sets goals for future encounters. Working as a team not only supports intimacy but can strengthen other aspects of your relationship.

My fiancé and I had an early moment of "constructive feedback" during our first date. After our first kiss, I playfully said, "Let's talk about my preferences. Slower, with at least two kisses before tongue." He responded with grace, repeated what I said, and asked, "Like this?" before going in for another kiss. His openness and willingness to adapt established a strong foundation for our communication, both sexual and non-sexual.

The Recipe for a Fulfilling Sex Life

You now have the ingredients for a successful sex life: understand your desires, embrace discomfort, and communicate openly. Remember, every recipe varies based on taste and preference, so your experiences will be uniquely yours. By being flexible, curious, and open, you can create fulfilling, intimate connections that evolve with you over time.

Chapter Seven

Becoming Me: Letting Go of Perfection to Embrace Growth and Authenticity

By Carley Symes, BSc (Hons), MBACP

A compassionate therapist who guides clients through healing, self-understanding, and the work of becoming who they truly are.

At 21, I found myself perched on the edge of my bed, surrounded by the familiar space of my childhood room—the same four walls I had known since I was 10. Once painted a bold, vibrant purple, they now glowed a soft pastel pink, a change I had made before leaving for university. The corners of my wardrobe still carried echoes of who I had been: Twilight posters from my fifteen-year-old self, Harry Potter posters from even earlier, and a rebellious collage of Greenday and My Chemical Romance from the year I turned sixteen. Folded among T-shirts with slogans I had long outgrown were fragments of identities I had tried on, discarded, and outgrown.

The drawers of my dressing table were cluttered with revision notes, old diaries, tangled hair clips, and the remnants of inexpensive makeup sets—the kind gifted by relatives at Christmas. That mirror had seen everything: the smudged glitter experiments, tear-streaked cheeks, exhausted eyes, and the evolving face of a girl trying to figure out who she was becoming. And now, at 21, it reflected a question that weighed heavily on me: *Who does this new job require me to be?*

I had carefully chosen my outfit the night before, as though preparing armor. A red jumper and checked trousers, bought on a rare shopping trip far from home, gave me a sense of bravery. Cleated gladiator sandals strapped tight around my feet felt both intimidating and empowering. A chunky necklace sat firmly at my throat, and my hair and makeup did their best to match the version of myself I wanted the world to see.

It was my first "proper" job. Technically, I hadn't even graduated yet, but the pressure to secure something respectable had become relentless. I had applied to over forty positions in desperation and received only a handful of interviews. At school, the advice had seemed so simple: *Go to university—employers will love it.* But reality proved more complicated.

Each interview had ended the same way: rejection. When I spoke honestly about wanting to support people, about my dream of becoming a counsellor, I was told I was "too academic" or "not committed enough." One manager wanted someone willing to give "everything" to the role. Another simply dismissed me for having aspirations beyond the job itself. With every "no," I learned to edit myself a little more.

Then came the interview where something shifted. This time, instead of shutting down my passion, they leaned into it. "You've got good emotional intelligence," they told me. I felt a spark of recognition—someone finally saw value in what I carried within me. It wasn't the counselling work I longed for, but it was something. It was validation. So I said yes, grateful simply to be wanted.

Looking back, I see how that moment became the start of something deeper: a commitment not just to a job, but to a new version of myself. I believed I needed to shed softness and vulnerability, to become tougher, sharper, less breakable. I told myself this was the way forward—to leave behind the girl who cared too much and instead step into someone who could not be hurt.

But reality had other plans. The job quickly demanded more than I had expected, and I gave more than I intended. I found myself emotionally entangled with colleagues, attached to the work, constantly bending beyond my own limits. At first, my boss's praise felt intoxicating—I was the "best thing since sliced bread." Yet slowly, the praise disappeared, replaced by criticism, sexism, and impossible standards. I worked harder and harder, desperate to earn back what I had once received, unable to see that I was chasing approval from someone who was mistreating me.

When I look back at that 21-year-old version of myself, I feel sadness. She believed admiration mattered more than her own discomfort. She thought resilience meant ignoring her boundaries. But of course, this didn't begin at 21. This pattern had been nurtured long before: the belief that others' opinions carried more weight than her own needs.

And this is where so many of us get caught. From childhood, we absorb lessons about our worth through the responses of those around us. Were our tears comforted—or dismissed? Did our joy spark connection—or irritation? Did fear earn us reassurance—or anger? Each interaction built a blueprint, teaching us which parts of ourselves were welcome and which parts were not.

As adults, it's easy to forget how much those early lessons still shape us. But the truth is, we all carry them. And if we don't question them, we risk repeating the same cycle I did at

21—trading authenticity for approval, boundaries for belonging.

Building Our Identity Blueprint

The ways our caregivers respond to us become the earliest building blocks of our identity. Every smile, sigh, or frown lands on us like a verdict about who we are. As children, we don't yet understand that our parents' or caregivers' reactions are shaped by *their* lives—their stress, moods, histories. To us, it all feels personal. As Gabor Maté explains, children are "narcissists in the developmental sense": everything is about us.

That's how we begin constructing a sense of self—not from the inside out, but from the reflections we see in others.

This doesn't necessarily come from neglect or abuse; even in loving families, these subtle moments leave a mark. Picture a child beaming at their mum, only to be met with blankness because she is weighed down by depression. Or a child who has lost their favorite toy, reaching out for comfort, but finding a father too consumed by work and guilt to join in the search. In both cases, the child is still loved. But what they take from those moments isn't about love—it's about whether their joy or sadness is acceptable.

And so we learn. We begin to hide or reshape feelings that don't seem welcomed. We lean into behaviors that earn praise or ease others' burdens. These become the early measuring sticks for our self-worth.

By adolescence, our circle of influence widens. We look beyond our parents for validation and take in thousands of subtle (and not so subtle) messages about who we should be. Some teens rebel, pushing against those childhood rules; others double down, perfecting their role as the caretaker, the achiever, the "good one." Often, both kinds live under the same roof, locked in their own tug-of-war for identity.

In today's digital age, this struggle has only intensified. On TV, a singer is celebrated for her pretty face. On Instagram, a prank video racks up a million likes. Influencers bare their lives online, absorbing thousands of comments as judgment. Magazines mock bodies; cancel culture punishes mistakes as though they're permanent.

Closer to home, friends climb social ladders, teachers signal approval or disapproval in subtle ways, peers decide who's "cool" and who's not. Layer upon layer, these messages weave themselves into our sense of self. And without even realizing it, they start to dictate what we believe is acceptable and what isn't.

By the time I was 21, sitting on the edge of that bed, I thought I had a clear picture of who I should become. I had already absorbed so many verdicts: the friends who had turned their backs on me, the bullies who convinced me I was the problem, the teachers who told me to stay quiet to avoid hurting someone else's feelings. The lesson seemed obvious: "good girls keep quiet and do as they are told

So I drew up a blueprint of the woman I thought I needed to be—strong, detached, immune to hurt, and never in need of approval. I believed if I could fix myself into that version, I would finally be safe.

Can I Really Fix Me?

Looking back, I see how wrong I was. The rejection and mistreatment I had endured didn't reflect my worth, but at the time I believed they did. I told myself: *I was weak. I let it happen. I need to be different.* What I didn't see was how often I had abandoned my own perspective to absorb someone else's. When people handed me their shame or self-hatred, I carried it as though it were mine.

Instead of realizing the mirror was cracked, I tried to fix the me I saw in my reflection. I searched for new "rules" to live by—rules that might guarantee acceptance, rules that might protect me from rejection. I believed if I could edit myself just right, I could finally control how people treated me.

But here's the truth: when we chase approval, we lose ourselves. We stop seeing through our own eyes and start seeing only through the imagined eyes of others. My self-perception shattered into distorted fragments, and the harder I tried to "fix" them, the more lost I became.

This is not just my story. It's a pattern I see in so many of the clients I work with. The quest to "find ourselves" often disguises itself as an attempt to *fix* ourselves. We think: *If I can get rid of the parts people don't like, I'll finally be okay.* Or we try to numb the part of us that even cares about others' opinions—forgetting that caring is an essential, human trait.

Fixing implies permanence. It says: *If I can change this one thing about myself, then I'll never struggle again.* But life doesn't work that way. Self-acceptance is not about erasing the parts we dislike—it's about learning to live with them, to hear what they're telling us.

Looking in the mirror and embracing only the parts you like is easy. True growth comes when you can face the parts you don't.

Seeing Ourselves Through Others' Eyes

Years later, even with the insight I've gained, I sometimes catch myself slipping back into old patterns—hearing the voice of a bully in my own inner critic. Once, my therapist observed: *"Do you realize you talk about yourself as if you're the bully describing you?"*

I hadn't realized. But it hit me deeply. When we adopt the perspective of those who harmed us, it becomes nearly impossible to see ourselves clearly, let alone kindly.

And that's the real challenge: learning to see ourselves through our own eyes, not theirs.

Fixing vs. Growing

We are constantly changing and evolving as individuals. But when we spend our energy trying to "fix" ourselves, it becomes nearly impossible to embrace who we truly are. Contentment begins when we stop treating imperfection as something shameful and start allowing it to be part of our humanity.

This doesn't mean we should ignore areas where growth is needed. Clear self-awareness allows us to notice the patterns and behaviors that hold us back. But there's an important distinction between *fixing* and *growing*.

Fixing starts with the assumption that something in us is wrong. We zero in on that flaw and imagine a perfect end state where the problem has been erased. We believe, *once I change this, I'll finally feel okay.*

Growth, by contrast, makes space for discomfort. It allows us to learn from those difficult emotions and integrate them into who we are becoming. Growth is not about reaching an endpoint; it's about developing a relationship with ourselves that allows for change, curiosity, and compassion along the way.

When we chase "fixing," we wait for a perfect version of ourselves before starting our goals. We think: *I'll take that trip once I feel confident. I'll go for that job when I'm sure of myself. I'll put myself out there when I feel strong enough to withstand scrutiny.*

But here's the paradox: confidence doesn't arrive *before* the action. It develops *through* the action.

Imagine you dream of a solo trip to Greece: warm beaches, a new language, fresh faces. Alongside the excitement comes fear—what if I get lost, what if I can't manage the logistics, what if I feel too alone? So you tell yourself, *I'll go once I'm confident enough.* But the longer you wait, the more unreachable the goal feels, until a year later you think, *If I couldn't do it then, I definitely can't do it now.*

What if you had gone without waiting for confidence? Each time you solved a problem—navigating a train delay, managing your budget, finding your way—you would build trust in yourself. Confidence isn't a prerequisite; it's the outcome of experience. It is a trust in ourselves that is built.

If we wait to be "fixed" before we live, we may never begin. Growth can only happen if we stop waiting to be perfect.

What Confidence Really Means

Many of us (my younger self included) confuse confidence with self-esteem. But confidence simply means *to trust.* It grows when we repeat tasks, face fears, and build evidence that we can handle what comes. It's not about becoming flawless; it's about building trust in our own resilience.

At 21, though, I didn't see it that way. I thought confidence meant becoming someone entirely different—stronger, louder, tougher. I saw myself as a pushover, and I believed my sensitivity was the problem. My plan was to fix it: bury the softness, enforce rigid boundaries, pretend I didn't care so deeply.

But pretending never works for long. I remember my boss asking me to take on extra work because they were struggling.

My façade of toughness crumbled instantly. I agreed, because beneath the armor I was still the same sensitive, caring person. And because I had been denying that truth, people found it easier to exploit it.

In rejecting sensitivity, I had actually stripped away the clarity I needed to communicate my needs. By pretending I wasn't soft, I silenced the signals that told me when something didn't feel right.

The same happened with my shyness. I decided it was a weakness and tried to cover it with forced confidence. But instead of making me stronger, it made me more fragile. I ignored the part of me that needed quiet, reflection, and gentleness—and in doing so, I built an even shakier foundation.

If you had called me a "people pleaser" back then, I would have denied it. "How could I be a people pleaser if I can't even seem to please people?" I would have joked. The irony is obvious now. My endless attempts to "get it right" for everyone else pulled me further away from myself- I was haunted by experiences I wasn't yet ready to admit had done damage outside of my control.

External Scripts and the Ideal Self

Looking back, I want to shake that girl sitting on the edge of the bed in her carefully chosen armor. She thought ignoring her sensitivity and pushing forward would protect her. She thought if she dressed the part, silenced her needs, and played the role of the "ideal self," she could outrun the ghosts of sadness, fear, and rejection.

But those shadows don't disappear when we slam the door on them. They wait. They grow louder.

My focus wasn't really on discovering *who I was*. It was on chasing *who I thought I should be*—a patchwork ideal stitched together from cultural messaging, admired figures, and all the things I had been told I was "wrong" for being.

YouTube creators told me how I should look. Magazines instructed me on how to be desirable and likable. Online quizzes promised to reveal "what kind of person I was" but left me feeling even more uncertain. And every time I followed the steps and still didn't feel the way I was promised, I blamed myself: *I must have done something wrong.*

This is the trap of external blueprints. They sell us an ideal version of ourselves while widening the gap between who we are and who we believe we should be. And in that gap, shame thrives.

From Childhood Messages to Adult Rules

You might have noticed certain words repeating throughout—messages we receive as children, influences in our teenage years. It's tempting to think that when we become adults, those lessons fade away. But the truth is, they follow us. They stay alive inside us if we still believe they keep us safe, if we think we need them to belong, if we're convinced they measure our worth.

In adulthood, these early messages often harden into rules—our personal “shoulds” and “shouldn’ts.”

As a child, I learned that crying “too much” or feeling “too deeply” drew disapproval. At school, I was rewarded for looking after others and punished for speaking out. Among friends, I noticed I got invited to more things if I let others be in control. These weren’t just moments; they were lessons about how to survive.

As a teenager, the pattern deepened. Teachers reassured my parents I was “no trouble,” while others who expressed emotions were reprimanded. I was praised for being mature, for not needing attention, for making life easier for everyone. At every stage, I absorbed the same core rule: put others first, and you will be safe- even though I had already experienced this not being true.

By the time I was 21, sitting on my bed in that carefully chosen outfit, I was already fluent in these rules. So when my new boss praised my ability to read people and asked me to use those skills to manage colleagues for their benefit, of course I said yes. It felt natural—it fit the script I had been rehearsing for years.

This is how rules form: through repetition. We learn what brings praise, what avoids punishment, what secures a little safety or lets us feel in control. Over time, those threads are woven tightly into our personality. Some of them we’re born with, some come from childhood, others from adolescence, but together they merge into a single tapestry.

So who was I then? Honestly, I couldn't have told you. When we dislike what we find inside, it's easier to focus on the outside—to fix the version of ourselves the world sees. But that kind of fixing is never sustainable.

The Complex Relationship Between Body and Identity

That's where many of us turn next: to our bodies. Our bodies are the most tangible representation of self—the part the world sees first. It feels logical to believe that if we change our appearance, we can change who we are, or at least how we're treated.

But our poor bodies often carry the weight of our identity struggles. I know mine did. Whenever my self-esteem dropped, my relationship with my body took the hit. At 21, it became the focus of my attempts to create a new identity and leave behind a self I had not yet come to validate as what she was traumatised.

We use clothes as armor—baggy clothes to hide, bold outfits to project confidence, makeup and styling to express sexuality or conceal insecurity. We sculpt, shrink, and reshape our bodies in pursuit of qualities we believe the changes will grant us: *When I'm thinner, I'll feel safe. When I'm sculpted, I'll feel healthy. When I'm perfect, I'll finally be worthy.*

The promises are alluring but false. Battle armor can influence how the world sees us, but when the armor comes off—alone, in front of the mirror—we're faced with the same questions.

Beyond our choices, some aspects of our bodies are inherited: skin color, features, build, gender markers. They shape how others categorize us and how we categorize ourselves. They influence belonging, connection, and identity labels.

For me, being "the pale one" in a family that tans easily felt like not fitting in. Dyeing my hair blonde, on the other hand, helped me feel more like myself and more visually connected to my mum and sister. Even these small details shaped my sense of belonging, revealing how intertwined body and identity can be.

But while our bodies are part of how we move through the world, they do not define who we are. They are vessels, not verdicts. As C.S. Lewis wrote: *"You don't have a soul. You are a soul. You have a body."*

Listening to the Self Beneath the Rules

Beyond our bodies, there are countless external markers—accents, hometowns, cultural influences—that shape how we're seen and how we see ourselves. For me, growing up in the southwest of England linked me to a culture of quietness, nature, and solitude. Rolling fields, spring lambs, woodland groves, and the sea shaped my rhythm. These surroundings don't define me, but they reveal what feels right to me—what grounds me, what soothes me.

And that's the point: these things are less about definition and more about direction. They are roots of connection, clues pointing us toward belonging.

Brené Brown draws the crucial distinction: *"Fitting in is about assessing a situation and becoming who you need to be to be accepted. Belonging doesn't require us to change who we are; it requires us to be who we are."*

When I pay attention to what makes me feel content, I notice where I belong and where I don't. A quiet walk, a nod from a passerby, the peace of not needing to perform—these moments tell me more about myself than any external rule ever could.

The challenge, of course, is letting go of the judgment. Thoughts creep in: *I should talk more. I should walk faster. I should be more observant.* These are the "shoulds" of the outside world, trying to drown out the truth. But when I let them go, even briefly, the contentment I feel pulls me back toward myself.

The Role of Feelings in Identity

Happiness is a guidepost—it shows us what aligns with our values. But so are other emotions. Sadness points to what matters. Anger signals when boundaries are crossed. Fear tells us where caution may be needed. Each feeling is a message, an inner compass pointing us toward who we are.

Identity is not about always being consistent. We change, we grow, and that is good. What we *can* be consistent with is listening—paying attention to our emotions and letting them guide us toward a truer understanding of ourselves.

Listening to Our Emotions

Anger has taught me where to stand my ground, where something clashes with my values or boundaries. Often, I notice it most when I've allowed those boundaries to bend too far. The resentment that creeps in is my signal: it's time to reset if the relationship is to continue in a healthy way.

For years, I ignored my anger, branding it "bad." But anger, like every feeling, carries a message. Welcoming it—not as good or bad, but simply as information—has helped me know myself more fully.

Sadness has sometimes felt overwhelming, like drowning in an ocean with no end. Yet when I've learned to listen to it, sadness has revealed itself as a guide to meaning. It tells me when I need gentleness, connection, and kindness. Without sadness, I lose touch with what truly matters. When I accept it, it hurts and it heals.

Fear, too, has its role. It warns me of danger, but it also shows me where I feel incapable, where I need to build trust in myself. Fear tells me I'm stepping outside my comfort zone—and reminds me to create safety alongside the risk. When I meet fear with compassion, it doesn't consume me. Instead, it becomes intuition, guiding rather than holding me back.

Listening without judgment is what transforms emotions from obstacles into teachers. Each one has something to say about who we are.

Acceptance vs. "Self-Love"

This raises a bigger question: if self-acceptance means welcoming all of our emotions, are we really talking about *self-love*?

The phrase "self-love" can feel heavy, even intimidating. Many people think it means we must love every part of ourselves, all the time. But the reality is—none of us do. And that's okay.

We don't have to adore every trait or feeling in order to know ourselves or live authentically. What matters is that we acknowledge them, listen to them, and stop treating them as permanent verdicts on our worth. We can hold love with clear-eyed insight, and temper self-criticism with acceptance.

That middle ground—acceptance without judgment—is what allows us to build a secure relationship with ourselves.

Letting Go of the Endpoint

So, are we any closer to answering the question: *Who am I?* Perhaps. But not in the way my 21-year-old self imagined.

Back then, I believed that once I figured out "who I was," life would finally become easy. Boundaries would come without guilt, decisions would flow effortlessly, and I would live from a steady, unshakable core. Like so many of us, I longed for an endpoint—a finished, polished version of myself that would make everything simpler.

But identity doesn't work that way. There is no final destination. We are flexible, changing beings. Even the feelings that seem most defining are fleeting—scientists say emotions last only about 90 seconds before shifting. How could we expect to be fixed, static, certain, when we are designed to evolve?

Clients often tell me they're waiting for confidence before taking the next step: *"I'll travel once I feel sure of myself. I'll apply for that job when I'm stronger. I'll share my work when I'm no longer vulnerable."* But what they're really longing for is freedom from discomfort. And while that desire makes sense, it isn't realistic. Growth *comes with* discomfort. Confidence doesn't eliminate vulnerability—it develops right beside it.

Knowing ourselves doesn't resolve every struggle. Life will still ask us to make hard choices, still throw us curveballs. But what changes is the way we relate to ourselves in those moments.

Asking Better Questions

Nearly five years after that day on the bed, I finally entered a space where I felt safe enough to explore myself. Sitting with the women I completed my final training alongside, I saw their vulnerability, their realness, and I began to give myself permission to do the same. With my therapist, and in my relationship, I discovered new questions—ones that mattered more than "Who am I?"

Who am I if I don't have to be what everyone else wants me to be?

Who can I be if my worth isn't tied to my utility?

Who am I when I listen to myself, without the filter of others' imagined perceptions?

These questions opened up space—for me to breathe, to listen, to belong to myself.

Making Space for the Whole Self

If we want to build a positive relationship with ourselves, the first step is simple but radical: make space.
Space to hear our feelings.
Space to notice what we want, what we like, what we don't.
Space to allow the less polished versions of ourselves into the light.

But making space isn't easy—especially when so many of us learned the opposite. We were taught, subtly or outright, that "good girls" don't take up space. They don't make noise, they don't disrupt, and they certainly don't leave an impact. Yet that is exactly what we must unlearn. Because giving ourselves permission to take up space, to speak, to exist fully and visibly, is the only way we can ever feel truly connected to who we are.

If we only ever present the "best" version of ourselves, the rest of us gets silenced. Those hidden parts miss the chance to be understood, challenged, accepted, or even loved. Growth happens only when every part of us is allowed into the daylight.

You don't have to wait until you're perfect to show up, take up space, or make choices. In fact, waiting for perfection keeps you from ever starting.

Think of the facets of your identity as melodies in a single song. Each part can be turned up or softened, changing the sound without ever losing the essence. New lines can be added, old ones can fade out over time, and harmonies you once relied on may evolve into something different. In this way, we can appreciate the evolution of our song—hearing every shift, every change—without expecting it to stay the same forever.

Trusting Ourselves

One lesson from my training has stayed with me: we can learn to trust ourselves as the foundation of our experience. That means listening to our feelings, considering the impact of our choices, and acting from the information we have in the present moment.

When our inner world and outer actions align, we experience congruence—a harmony between what we feel inside and what we show outside. That congruence is one of the deepest sources of confidence.

But to reach it, we must first create safe spaces—inside ourselves and in our relationships—where we can hear our own voices clearly. From there, we can choose where to invest our energy, who to invite into our lives, and how to stand in alignment with who we are becoming. To me, this reflects the importance of listening to our instincts and deciding which people we do and don't want to invest ourselves into.

Coming Home to Myself

My body, my face, and my mind continue to change as time goes by—and what a privilege it is to keep learning myself, to meet new versions of me, and to allow space for them. The more I have stopped trying to fix myself, the more comfortable I've become in who I am. The more I've accepted that I am not one permanent version, the more I've been able to release the grip of perfection. We are changing and growing, and thank goodness that we are.

The mirror that once sat on the dressing table in my childhood bedroom now sits in my new home. Since that day at 21, it has witnessed so many versions of me. New tears and new hopes after university. New laughter as I fell in love. Moving vans and first-day outfits as I tried on different jobs, fighting to carve out the one I really wanted. At times, I even turned it to face the wall, afraid of what it might reflect back. It has seen scars, recoveries, friendships, and fresh beginnings. Now it sees me sitting here writing, tentatively adding *writer, storyteller* (my fear still whispers *oversharer*) to the list of selves I am trying on. I'll see how it feels.

Earlier, we talked about "shoulds and shouldn'ts." What are yours? These rules often masquerade as safety but keep us disconnected from ourselves. They can lower confidence, because when we rely on external rules instead of our own feelings, we place trust outside rather than within. Building confidence and self-esteem means listening to that inner voice—valuing its opinion at least as much as those external "shoulds."

Letting go of these rules is hard. They offer conditional validation, and that can feel safer than stepping into the unknown. My 21-year-old self wasn't ready to release them. She still believed the approval of others was worth the sacrifice of authenticity. But that kind of validation was never enough—it was always too fragile to build a life on.

Being valued by others feels good, but if it comes at the cost of betraying or hiding our authentic self, it erodes genuine self-worth. Accepting ourselves is not a finish line. It's a slow, ongoing process. There will always be triggers. Some days acceptance comes easily, other days it's a struggle. That's part of being human.

Because we are not fixed. We are not one thing. I was me when I had the Harry Potter poster on my wall, when I dyed a purple stripe into my hair, when I was scolded for daydreaming in class, and when I was awarded for my writing. I was me when I said something unkind I regretted, and I was me when I held my friend as she cried.

The more I release the idea of a perfect, permanent version of myself, the freer I feel. We are always becoming, always unfolding. And when I lose sight of myself—as I still sometimes do—I know how to find my way back. I return to the things that feel like home: slow walks, thick fruit smoothies, cozy blankets, quiet companionship. Warm hugs and cold air. These small things are my map—back to the places I can reconnect with myself, to the old me, the present me, and the next me.

The next me, intertwined with the existing me, holding hands with the girl on the bed.

Chapter Eight

About the Authors

Chapter 1: Mapping Mental Health: A Journey with a Guide

Dr. Joshua Bess, MD, is a compassionate psychiatrist and educator dedicated to helping individuals navigate their mental health journeys. With expertise in treatment-resistant mood disorders, catatonia, and brain stimulation therapies like ECT, he is passionate about thoughtful, individualized care. Dr. Bess combines evidence-based pharmacotherapy with a patient-centered approach, guiding clients through complex treatment decisions.

An accomplished author, Dr. Bess co-wrote the *Manual of Inpatient Psychiatry* and has contributed to numerous scholarly articles. He has also held leadership roles, including President of the Washington State Psychiatric Association (2019–2020), and remains committed to advancing mental health care and education.

Chapter 2: Helping Others Heal from Loss: Navigating Grief and Rebuilding Hope

Jane Anderson, MFS, CFLE combines over 40 years of experience in healthcare and education to create powerful community wellness programs. With a background in patient care and crisis intervention, she has dedicated her life to helping others. Armed with a master's degree in Family Studies, Jane is passionate about teaching and empowering communities. Her dynamic trainings on mental health, family dynamics, and wellness have reached thousands, making a lasting impact. Whether she's leading a workshop or developing new programs, Jane is committed to uplifting others. . Her journey from the medical professional to community advocate continues to inspire and transform lives.

Chapter 3: Recipe for a Fulfilling Sex Life: Getting Comfortable with Sex Being Uncomfortable

Dr. Randi Reichel Fournier, DMFT, LMFT, M.Ed. is a therapist, relationship coach, and author dedicated to helping individuals and couples navigate the complexities of sexual health and relationships. Combining advanced training with clinical expertise, she specializes in fostering open communication, emotional intimacy, and personal growth. Dr. Fournier is passionate about breaking down societal stigmas and normalizing conversations around intimacy, creating a safe space for exploring desires and overcoming challenges. Known for her relatable, evidence-based approach infused with humor and vulnerability, she empowers clients and readers to embrace self-awareness and build meaningful, fulfilling connections in their relationships and personal lives.

Chapter 4: The Labyrinth of Toxic Love: Recognizing and Reclaiming Yourself

Nina Batista, MSW, is a dedicated counselor specializing in helping individuals recognize and heal from toxic relationships and emotional abuse. With a foundation in psychology and a Master of Social Work from Florida Atlantic University, Nina brings a trauma-informed approach to therapy, blending empathy with honest, direct feedback. She is certified in treating survivors of coercive control, narcissistic abuse, and gaming addiction, among other specialties.

Nina's therapeutic approach integrates CBT, DBT, Gestalt, and Attachment Theory, crafting personalized treatment plans that empower clients to reclaim their identity and well-being. She is passionate about fostering trust and growth in her clients' journeys to healing.

Chapter 5: Becoming Me: Letting Go of Perfection to Embrace Growth and Authenticity

Carley Symes, BSc (Hons), MBACP (Registered Member), is a humanistic integrative therapist dedicated to fostering self-acceptance and personal growth. With a deep understanding of mental health rooted in her BPS-accredited psychology degree and counseling qualifications, Carley combines evidence-based theories to create a safe, adaptive space for clients. She draws on her personal journey of overcoming self-esteem challenges to connect authentically with those she supports. Carley's approach emphasizes compassion, self-discovery, and building resilience, guiding individuals toward positive change and fulfillment.

Chapter 6: The Journey to Self-Love: Becoming Your Own Best Friend

Joelle Maletis, MAEd, MA, LMFT, is a renowned psychotherapist, trauma expert, and advocate for self-love and resilience. Drawing from years of experience, Joelle empowers individuals to embrace their imperfections and rediscover their inner strength. Her transformative TED-Ed video on PTSD has reached over 3.2 million viewers worldwide and is used to train AI in 28 languages.

As an international speaker and executive coach, Joelle inspires others to overcome adversity and build fulfilling lives. Founder of JRM&A Inc., she combines therapeutic expertise with entrepreneurial insights, helping people thrive despite challenges. Joelle's compassionate approach continues to impact lives globally.

Chapter Nine

Thank You

As we come to the end of this anthology, it is important to pause and recognize what it truly means to arrive here. Reading about mental health is not passive work. It is emotional labor, introspection, and often a form of gentle disruption. It invites you to reconsider old beliefs, soften long-held defenses, and look honestly at the parts of yourself you have protected, hidden, or forgotten. You have done something meaningful by opening these pages and allowing them to meet you where you are. For that, we want to say thank you.

Thank you for choosing yourself.
Thank you for choosing your healing.
Thank you for choosing to understand your mind, your story, and your emotions more deeply.

This book was created with a simple intention. To offer clarity, compassion, and connection in a world that often expects people to hold their pain silently. Mental health has long been tangled in stigma, misunderstanding, and the pressure to appear "fine." But every reader who picks up a book like this helps move the world forward. Every person who chooses to learn, explore, or question the patterns shaping their well-being contributes to a much larger cultural shift. Healing becomes possible when individuals make mental health a priority, not only for themselves but for the generations that follow.

To the readers who came to these pages seeking guidance, comfort, or validation, we honor the courage it took to arrive here. Many people turn to mental health resources during times of uncertainty, grief, transition, or quiet inner struggle. Others turn to them from a place of growth, resilience, or curiosity. No matter what brought you here, your willingness to engage with these ideas is an act of self-love. It is a declaration that your inner world deserves care and understanding. It is a reminder that healing is not something you must earn. It is something you deserve simply because you exist.

We also extend heartfelt gratitude to the contributors of this anthology. Each author brought a lifetime of experience, professional dedication, and personal humanity to these chapters. Their roles in the mental health field place them on the front lines of human emotion. Day after day, they sit with people in their most vulnerable moments, listen to stories shaped by pain and hope, and offer tools that help transform lives. The insights they share in this book come not only from academic training or clinical expertise but from witnessing the real, complex journeys of healing that unfold in the therapy room, in the psychiatrist's office, in community centers, in family conversations, and in the quiet courage of individuals doing the work to become whole.

This anthology exists because these contributors believe deeply in the power of education and storytelling. They understand that mental health improves when knowledge is accessible, when compassion is extended freely, and when people are given permission to explore their inner world without shame. Their voices help illuminate pathways that can feel overwhelming to walk alone. They remind us that healing is possible, that support exists, and that every person carries within them the capacity to grow, rebuild, and reclaim their well-being.

To the professionals, educators, researchers, therapists, psychiatrists, and advocates who will read this anthology, thank you for your work. Your dedication shapes the landscape of mental health and directly impacts the lives of countless individuals who rely on your skill and compassion. This book is a reflection of the collective heartbeat of your field, a reminder that the work you do continues to ripple outward in ways that cannot always be seen but are always felt.

To the friends, family members, partners, caretakers, and supporters of those experiencing mental health challenges, thank you for showing up. Thank you for listening, for learning, and for offering patience and empathy. Healing does not happen in isolation. It is nurtured in relationships that give space for honesty, struggle, and growth. Your role matters more than you may ever fully realize.

And to every reader who feels alone in their journey, we want to leave you with this. You are not alone. Even in your quietest struggles. Even in the moments you doubt your strength. Even in the seasons when healing feels slow or progress feels invisible. You are part of a larger human story, one in which millions of people are learning, just like you, how to take care of themselves in deeper and more compassionate ways.

The end of this book is not the end of your journey. It is an invitation to continue. To take what resonated with you and carry it forward in whatever way feels meaningful. To ask new questions. To seek support when needed. To let yourself rest when your body asks for rest. To acknowledge your emotions without judgment. To practice the slow, intentional act of choosing yourself again and again.

Healing is rarely dramatic. It is found in the small choices you make each day. Choosing to breathe. Choosing to understand. Choosing to speak kindly to yourself. Choosing to reach out. Choosing to hope. Choosing to believe that change is possible. These choices shape your life more than any single moment ever could.

As you step beyond these pages, may you feel supported, inspired, and strengthened. May you remember that mental health is not a destination but a continuous relationship with your own well-being. May you move through the world with greater compassion for yourself and others. And may the courage you showed by reading this book be a reminder of the resilience that lives within you.

Thank you for being here. Thank you for choosing healing. Thank you for choosing you.

Chapter Ten

Bibliography

American College of Obstetricians and Gynecologists. (n.d.). Sexual health. ACOG. https://www.acog.org/womens-health/faqs/sexual-health

American Psychiatric Association. (1994). Decade of the Brain. Retrieved from https://www.psychiatry.org

Arabi, S. (2016). Becoming the narcissist's nightmare: How to devalue and discard the narcissist while supplying yourself. SCW Archer Publishing.

Bancroft, L. (2003). Why does he do that? Inside the minds of angry and controlling men. Berkley Books.

Boss, P. (2006). Loss, trauma, and resilience: Therapeutic work with ambiguous loss. W.W. Norton.

Breznitz, S. (1984). Cry wolf: The psychology of false alarms. Lawrence Erlbaum Associates.

Brown, B. (2017). Braving the wilderness: The quest for true belonging and the courage to stand alone. Random House.

Brown, S. L. (2009). Women who love psychopaths: Inside the relationships of inevitable harm. Mask Publishing.

Carnes, P. (1997). The betrayal bond: Breaking free of exploitive relationships. Health Communications, Inc.

Cloud, H., & Townsend, J. (2017). Boundaries: When to say yes, how to say no to take control of your life (Updated and expanded ed.). Zondervan.

Gottman, J. M., & Gottman, J. S. (2019). Eight dates: Essential conversations for a lifetime of love. Workman Publishing.

Healy, D. (1997). The antidepressant era. Harvard University Press.

Herman, J. L. (2015). Trauma and recovery: The aftermath of violence—from domestic abuse to political terror (Rev. ed.). Basic Books.

Kübler-Ross, E., & Kessler, D. (2005). On grief and grieving: Finding the meaning of grief through the five stages of loss. Scribner.

Lehmiller, J. J. (2018). Tell me what you want: The science of sexual desire and how it can help you improve your sex life. Da Capo Press.

Linehan, M. M. (2015). DBT skills training manual (2nd ed.). Guilford Press.

Maté, G., & Maté, D. (2022). The myth of normal: Trauma, illness, and healing in a toxic culture. Avery.

Nagoski, E. (2015). Come as you are: The surprising new science that will transform your sex life. Simon & Schuster.

Neff, K. (2011). Self-compassion: The proven power of being kind to yourself. William Morrow.

Perel, E. (2006). Mating in captivity: Unlocking erotic intelligence. HarperCollins.

Roberts, A. R. (2005). Crisis intervention handbook: Assessment, treatment, and research (3rd ed.). Oxford University Press.

Rogers, C. R. (1961). On becoming a person: A therapist's view of psychotherapy. Houghton Mifflin.

Ryan, R. M., & Deci, E. L. (2017). Self-determination theory: Basic psychological needs in motivation, development, and wellness. Guilford Press.

Shorter, E. (1997). A history of psychiatry: From the era of the asylum to the age of Prozac. John Wiley & Sons.

Stroebe, M., Schut, H., & Boerner, K. (2017). Cautioning health-care professionals: Bereavement in the time of COVID-19. Omega: Journal of Death and Dying, 82(1), 23–42.

Tedeschi, R. G., & Calhoun, L. G. (2004). Posttraumatic growth: Conceptual foundations and empirical evidence. Psychological Inquiry, 15(1), 1–18.

van der Kolk, B. A. (2014). The body keeps the score: Brain, mind, and body in the healing of trauma. Viking.

Whitaker, R. (2002). Mad in America: Bad science, bad medicine, and the enduring mistreatment of the mentally ill. Perseus Publishing.

Worden, J. W. (2018). Grief counseling and grief therapy: A handbook for the mental health practitioner (5th ed.). Springer Publishing.

www.ingramcontent.com/pod-product-compliance
Lightning Source LLC
La Vergne TN
LVHW011510220926
848484LV00024B/793
* 9 7 9 8 3 4 8 2 9 7 5 5 8 *